The Study Catechism: Full Version

Witherspoon Press
Louisville, Kentucky

Book design by Carol Eberhart Johnson

Published by Witherspoon Press, a Ministry of the General Assembly Council, Congregational Ministries Publishing, Presbyterian Church (U.S.A.), Louisville, Kentucky

Printed in the United States of America

05 06 07 08 09 —10 9 8 7 6 5 4 3 2

Library of Congress Cataloging-in-Publication Data

The study catechism : full version.
p. cm.
ISBN 1-57153-038-X
1. Presbyterian Church (U.S.A.)—Catechisms. 2. Christian education of adults. I. Witherspoon Press.
BX8969.5.S78 2003
238'.5137—dc21

2003007285

Introduction

Catechisms may seem hopelessly out of date, suggesting rote memorization of abstract answers to questions no one is asking. We live in the Internet age, not the era of McGuffey's Readers! We belong to a church of open inquiry, not one of pat answers! Catechisms may seem to be relics of an educational era that, thankfully, is in the past. Why, then, did the Presbyterian Church (U.S.A.) approve three new catechisms in 1998, and why are they being published for use in Presbyterian congregations and homes?

Catechisms have been part of Reformed church life since the sixteenth-century Reformation. Three catechisms are included in the *Book of Confessions*—the Heidelberg Catechism, and the Westminster Larger and Shorter Catechisms. They were not meant to be memorized (that was a nineteenth-century "innovation"), but rather to be used as brief summaries of Christian faith and life, presented in dialogue form. Reformed catechisms have helped generations of Christians to explore the Apostles' Creed, the Ten Commandments, and the Lord's Prayer by posing honest questions and providing faithful and relevant answers.

The Heidelberg Catechism's teaching on the Ten Commandments is as suggestive today as it was 450 years ago. A good example is the series of questions and answers on the sixth commandment, "You shall not kill."

> **Q: What does God require in the sixth commandment?**
>
> A: That I am not to abuse, hate, injure, or kill my neighbor, either with thought, or by word or gesture, much less by deed, whether by myself or through another, but to lay aside all desire for revenge; and that I do not harm myself or willingly expose myself to danger. This is why the authorities are armed with the means to prevent murder.

> **Q: But does this commandment speak only of killing?**
>
> A: In forbidding murder God means to teach us that he abhors the root of murder, which is envy, hatred, anger, and desire for revenge, and that he regards all these as hidden murder.
>
> **Q: Is it enough, then, if we do not kill our neighbor in any of these ways?**
>
> A: No; for when God condemns envy, hatred, and anger, he requires us to love our neighbor as ourselves, to show patience, peace, gentleness, mercy, and friendliness toward him, to prevent injury to him as much as we can, also to do good to our enemies.

Notice how the catechism gives depth to the commandment, drawing upon the richness of Old Testament wisdom about the Law and New Testament teaching about love for neighbors. Notice, too, how the questions and answers move toward a positive appropriation of the commandment, pointing us beyond prohibitions and toward discipleship. Heidelberg's answers raise other questions, of course. And that is precisely the point! Catechisms are not intended to be the final word but the opening exchanges in a dialogue of faith that carries the conversation broader and deeper.

Catechisms can be a valuable part of catechesis—the ongoing process of instruction that is central to the formation of faith and faithfulness in the lives of believers. Faith formation, even in formal educational settings, is a rich process that employs a wide variety of methods and resources. Catechisms are not the only educational means at the church's disposal, but they are a valuable way of initiating a two-way conversation about Christian faith and life.

The new catechisms of the Presbyterian Church (U.S.A.) are designed for persons of different ages.

Belonging to God: A First Catechism is intended for children, beginning in the third or fourth grade. It departs from the traditional catechism format (Creed, Commandments, Lord's Prayer) and follows the general contours of the biblical narrative. Scripture verses are correlated with each question and answer. Belonging to God helps children understand the Bible in its relationship to God's love and our lives.

The Study Catechism: Full Version is intended for adults and older adolescents. It is suitable for study by new members of the church, college groups, adults in study groups, and church officers, in a variety of settings. Following the traditional format, the catechism strives to balance theological depth and accessibility.

The Study Catechism: Confirmation Version is a somewhat briefer and simpler version of The Study Catechism, suitable for use with confirmation classes composed of early adolescents.

These new catechisms are not "updates" of the church's earlier catechisms, but they do respond to contemporary concerns. The Study Catechism includes explorations of religious pluralism, science and faith, the shape of mission, and other pertinent issues, all in the context of basic Christian affirmations. The intention throughout is to acknowledge real questions and provide honest Christian answers in a way that encourages continued exploration.

The new Presbyterian Catechisms, used in whole or in part, can be an engaging means to enrich the educational ministry of the church, drawing children, youth, and adults into conversation with the whole church about believing and living as Christ's people in a world that hungers for the good news.

Joseph D. Small
Associate Director
Theology Worship and Discipleship
Presbyterian Church (U.S.A.)

The Study Catechism: Full Version

Question 1. What is God's purpose for your life?

God wills that I should live by the grace of the Lord Jesus Christ, for the love of God, and in the communion of the Holy Spirit.

> *2 Cor. 13:13* The grace of the Lord Jesus Christ, the love of God, and the communion of the Holy Spirit be with all of you.

Question 2. How do you live by the grace of the Lord Jesus Christ?

I am not my own. I have been bought with a price. The Lord Jesus Christ loved me and gave himself for me. I entrust myself completely to his care, giving thanks each day for his wonderful goodness.

> *1 Cor. 6:19–20* Or do you not know that your body is a temple of the Holy Spirit within you, which you have from God, and that you are not your own? For you were bought with a price; therefore glorify God in your body.

> *Gal. 2:20* It is no longer I who live, but it is Christ who lives in me. And the life I now live in the flesh I live by faith in the Son of God, who loved me and gave himself for me.

> *Ps. 136:1* O give thanks to the LORD, for he is good, for his steadfast love endures forever.

Question 3. How do you live for the love of God?

I love because God first loved me. God loves me in Christ with a love that never ends. Amazed by grace, I no longer live for myself. I live for the Lord who died and rose again, triumphant over death, for my sake. Therefore, I take those around me to heart, especially those in particular need, knowing that Christ died for them no less than for me.

1 John 4:19 We love because he first loved us.

2 Cor. 5:15 And he died for all, so that those who live might live no longer for themselves, but for him who died and was raised for them.

Rom. 12:15–16 Rejoice with those who rejoice, weep with those who weep. Live in harmony with one another; do not be haughty, but associate with the lowly; do not claim to be wiser than you are.

Question 4. How do you live in the communion of the Holy Spirit?

By the Holy Spirit, I am made one with the Lord Jesus Christ. I am baptized into Christ's body, the church, along with all others who confess him by faith. As a member of this community, I trust in God's Word, share in the Lord's Supper, and turn to God constantly in prayer. As I grow in grace and knowledge, I am led to do the good works that God intends for my life.

1 Cor. 12:27 Now you are the body of Christ and individually members of it.

Gal. 3:27 As many of you as were baptized into Christ have clothed yourselves with Christ.

1 Cor. 6:17, 19 But anyone united to the Lord becomes one spirit with him. . . . Or do you not know that your body is a temple of the Holy Spirit within you, which you have from God, and that you are not your own?

2 Peter 3:18 But grow in the grace and knowledge of our Lord and Savior Jesus Christ. To him be the glory both now and to the day of eternity. Amen.

Eph. 2:10 For we are what he has made us, created in Christ Jesus for good works, which God prepared beforehand to be our way of life.

I. The Apostles' Creed

Question 5. What does a Christian believe?

All that is promised in the gospel. A summary is found in the Apostles' Creed, which affirms the main content of the Christian faith.

> *John 20:31* But these are written so that you may come to believe that Jesus is the Messiah, the Son of God, and that through believing you may have life in his name.

Question 6. What is the first article of the Apostles' Creed?

> "I believe in God the Father Almighty, Maker of heaven and earth."

Question 7. What do you believe when you confess your faith in "God the Father Almighty"?

That God is a God of love, and that God's love is powerful beyond measure.

> *Lam. 3:22* The steadfast love of the LORD never ceases, his mercies never come to an end.

> *Song 8:7* Many waters cannot quench love, neither can floods drown it. If one offered for love all the wealth of one's house, it would be utterly scorned.

> *1 John 4:8* Whoever does not love does not know God, for God is love.

Question 8. How do you understand the love and power of God?

Through Jesus Christ. In his life of compassion, his death on the cross, and his resurrection from the dead, I see how vast is God's love for the world—a love that is ready to suffer for our sakes, yet so strong that nothing will prevail against it.

> *John 3:16* For God so loved the world that he gave his only Son, so that everyone who believes in him may not perish but may have eternal life.

Heb. 1:3 He is the reflection of God's glory and the exact imprint of God's very being, and he sustains all things by his powerful word.

1 John 4:9 God's love was revealed among us in this way: God sent his only Son into the world so that we might live through him.

Matt. 9:36 When he saw the crowds, he had compassion for them, because they were harassed and helpless, like sheep without a shepherd.

Ps. 106:8 Yet he saved them for his name's sake, so that he might make known his mighty power.

Question 9. What comfort do you receive from this truth?

This powerful and loving God is the one whose promises I may trust in all the circumstances of my life, and to whom I belong in life and in death.

Ps. 12:6 The promises of the LORD are promises that are pure, silver refined in a furnace on the ground, purified seven times.

Rom. 8:38–39 For I am convinced that neither death, nor life, nor angels, nor rulers, nor things present, nor things to come, nor powers, nor height, nor depth, nor anything else in all creation, will be able to separate us from the love of God in Christ Jesus our Lord.

Question 10. Do you make this confession only as an individual?

No. With the apostles, prophets, and martyrs, with all those through the ages who have loved the Lord Jesus Christ, and with all who strive to serve him on earth here and now, I confess my faith in the God of loving power and powerful love.

Heb. 12:1 Therefore, since we are surrounded by so great a cloud of witnesses, let us also lay aside every weight and the sin that clings so closely, and let us run with perseverance the race that is set before us. . . .

Rom. 1:12 . . . so that we may be mutually encouraged by each other's faith, both yours and mine.

Question 11. When the creed speaks of "God the Father," does it mean that God is male?

No. Only creatures having bodies can be either male or female. But God has no body, since by nature God is Spirit. Holy Scripture reveals God as a living God beyond all sexual distinctions. Scripture uses diverse images for God, female as well as male. We read, for example, that God will no more forget us than a woman can forget her nursing child (Isa. 49:15). "'As a mother comforts her child, so will I comfort you,' says the Lord" (Isa. 66:13).

Isa. 49:15 Can a woman forget her nursing child, or show no compassion for the child of her womb? Even these may forget, yet I will not forget you.

Isa. 66:13 As a mother comforts her child, so I will comfort you; you shall be comforted in Jerusalem.

Matt. 23:37 Jerusalem, Jerusalem, the city that kills the prophets and stones those who are sent to it! How often have I desired to gather your children together as a hen gathers her brood under her wings, and you were not willing!

Question 12. Why then does the creed speak of God the Father?

First, because God is identified in the New Testament as the Father of our Lord Jesus Christ. Second, because Jesus Christ is the eternal Son of this Father. Third, because when we are joined to Christ through faith, we are adopted as sons and daughters into the relationship he enjoys with his Father.

Rom. 1:7 To all God's beloved in Rome, who are called to be saints: Grace to you and peace from God our Father and the Lord Jesus Christ.

John 14:9-10 Jesus said to him, "Have I been with you all this time, Philip, and you still do not know me? Whoever has seen me has seen the Father. How can you say, 'Show us the Father'? Do you not believe that I am in the Father and the Father is in me? The words that I say to you I do not speak on my own; but the Father who dwells in me does his works."

John 17:24 Father, I desire that those also, whom you have given me, may be with me where I am, to see my glory, which you have given me because you loved me before the foundation of the world.

John 1:12 To all who received him, who believed in his name, he gave power to become children of God. . . .

Gal. 4:6 And because you are children, God has sent the Spirit of his Son into our hearts, crying, "Abba! Father!"

Question 13. When you confess the God and Father of our Lord Jesus Christ, are you elevating men over women and endorsing male domination?

No. Human power and authority are trustworthy only as they reflect God's mercy and kindness, not abusive patterns of domination. As Jesus taught his disciples, "The greatest among you will be your servant" (Matt. 23:11). God the Father sets the standard by which all misuses of power are exposed and condemned. "Call no one your father on earth," said Jesus, "for you have one Father—the one in heaven" (Matt. 23:9). In fact God calls women and men to all ministries of the church.

Gal. 3:28 There is no longer Jew or Greek, there is no longer slave or free, there is no longer male and female; for all of you are one in Christ Jesus.

Eph. 5:21 Be subject to one another out of reverence for Christ.

Question 14. If God's love is powerful beyond measure, why is there so much evil in the world?

No one can say why, for evil is a terrible abyss beyond all rational explanation. Its ultimate origin is obscure. Its enormity perplexes us. Nevertheless, we boldly affirm that God's triumph over evil is certain. In Jesus Christ God suffers with us, knowing all our sorrows. In raising him from the dead, God gives new hope to the world. Our Lord Jesus Christ, crucified and risen, is himself God's promise that suffering will come to an end, that death shall be no more, and that all things will be made new.

Ps. 23:4 Even though I walk through the darkest valley, I fear no evil; for you are with me; your rod and your staff—they comfort me.

1 Peter 1:3 Blessed be the God and Father of our Lord Jesus Christ! By his great mercy he has given us a new birth into a living hope through the resurrection of Jesus Christ from the dead.

2 Peter 3:13 But, in accordance with his promise, we wait for new heavens and a new earth, where righteousness is at home.

Rom. 8:21 The creation itself will be set free from its bondage to decay and will obtain the freedom of the glory of the children of God.

Job 19:25 For I know that my Redeemer lives, and that at the last he will stand upon the earth. . . .

Question 15. What do you believe when you say that God is "Maker of heaven and earth"?

First, that God called heaven and earth, with all that is in them, into being out of nothing simply by the power of God's Word. Second, that by that same power all things are upheld and governed in perfect wisdom, according to God's eternal purpose.

Rev. 4:11 You are worthy, our Lord and God, to receive glory and honor and power, for you created all things, and by your will they existed and were created.

Gen. 1:1 In the beginning when God created the heavens and the earth, and the earth was a formless void and darkness covered the face of the deep, while a wind from God swept over the face of the waters.

Heb. 11:3 By faith we understand that the worlds were prepared by the word of God, so that what is seen was made from things that are not visible.

Question 16. What does it mean to say that we human beings are created in the image of God?

That God created us to live together in love and freedom—with God, with one another, and with the world. Our distinctive capacities—reason, imagination, volition and so on—are given primarily for this purpose. We are created to be loving companions of others so that something of God's goodness may be reflected in our lives.

Gen. 1:26 Then God said, "Let us make humankind in our image, according to our likeness; and let them have dominion over the fish of the sea, and over the birds of the air, and over the cattle, and over all the wild animals of the earth, and over every creeping thing that creeps upon the earth."

Gen. 1:27 So God created humankind in his image, in the image of God he created them; male and female he created them.

Question 17. What does our creation in God's image reflect about God's reality?

Our being created in and for relationship is a reflection of the Holy Trinity. In the mystery of the one God, the three divine persons—Father, Son and Holy Spirit—live in, with and for one another eternally in perfect love and freedom.

Luke 3:21–22 Now when all the people were baptized, and when Jesus also had been baptized and was praying, the heaven was opened, and the Holy Spirit descended upon him in bodily form like a dove. And a voice came from heaven, "You are my Son, the Beloved; with you I am well pleased."

John 1:18 No one has ever seen God. It is God the only Son, who is close to the Father's heart, who has made him known.

John 5:19 Jesus said to them, "Very truly, I tell you, the Son can do nothing on his own, but only what he sees the Father doing; for whatever the Father does, the Son does likewise."

John 17:21–22 As you, Father, are in me and I am in you, may they also be in us, so that the world may believe that you have sent me. The glory that you have given me I have given them, so that they may be one, as we are one. . . .

Question 18. What does our creation in God's image reflect about God's love for us?

We are created to live wholeheartedly for God. When we honor our Creator as the source of all good things, we are like mirrors reflecting back the great beam of love that God shines on us. We are also created to honor God by showing love toward other human beings.

Ps. 9:1 I will give thanks to the LORD with my whole heart; I will tell of all your wonderful deeds.

1 John 4:7 Beloved, let us love one another, because love is from God; everyone who loves is born of God and knows God.

1 John 4:11 Beloved, since God loved us so much, we also ought to love one another.

Matt. 5:14–16 You are the light of the world. A city built on a hill cannot be hid. No one after lighting a lamp puts it under the bushel basket, but on the lampstand, and it gives light to all in the house. In the same way, let your light shine before others, so that they may see your good works and give glory to your Father in heaven.

Question 19. As creatures made in God's image, what responsibility do we have for the earth?

God commands us to care for the earth in ways that reflect God's loving care for us. We are responsible for ensuring that earth's gifts be used fairly and wisely, that no creature suffers from the abuse of what we are given, and that future generations may continue to enjoy the abundance and goodness of the earth in praise to God.

Ps. 24:1 The earth is the LORD's and all that is in it, the world, and those who live in it. . . .

Ps. 89:11 The heavens are yours, the earth also is yours; the world and all that is in it—you have founded them.

Gen. 2:15 The LORD God took the man and put him in the garden of Eden to till it and keep it.

Gen. 1:26 Then God said, "Let us make humankind in our image, according to our likeness; and let them have dominion over the fish of the sea, and over the birds of the air, and over the cattle, and over all the wild animals of the earth, and over every creeping thing that creeps upon the earth."

Isa. 24:5 The earth lies polluted under its inhabitants; for they have transgressed laws, violated the statutes, broken the everlasting covenant.

Rom. 12:2 Do not be conformed to this world, but be transformed by the renewing of your minds, so that you may discern the will of God—what is good and acceptable and perfect.

Question 20. Was the image of God lost when we turned from God by falling into sin?

Yes and no. Sin means that all our relations with others have become distorted and confused. Although we did not cease to be with God, our fellow human beings, and other creatures, we did cease to be for them; and although we did not lose our distinctive human capacities completely, we did lose the ability to use them rightly, especially in relation to God. Having ruined our connection with God by disobeying God's will, we are persons with hearts curved in upon ourselves. We have become slaves to the sin of which we are guilty, helpless to save ourselves, and are free, so far as freedom remains, only within the bounds of sin.

John 8:34 Jesus answered them, "Very truly, I tell you, everyone who commits sin is a slave to sin."

Rom. 3:23 All have sinned and fall short of the glory of God. . . .

Rom. 3:10 There is no one who is righteous, not even one. . . .

Rom. 1:21 Though they knew God, they did not honor him as God or give thanks to him, but they became futile in their thinking, and their senseless minds were darkened.

Isa. 59:1–3 See, the LORD's hand is not too short to save, nor his ear too dull to hear. Rather, your iniquities have been barriers between you and your God, and your sins have hidden his face from you so that he does not hear. For your hands are defiled with blood, and your fingers with iniquity; your lips have spoken lies, your tongue mutters wickedness.

Question 21. What does it mean to say that Jesus Christ is the image of God?

Despite our turning from God, God did not turn from us, but instead sent Jesus Christ in the fullness of time to restore our broken humanity. Jesus lived completely for God, by giving himself completely for us, even to the point of dying for us. By living so completely for others, he manifested what he was—the perfect image of God. When by grace we are conformed to him through faith, our humanity is renewed according to the divine image that we lost.

Isa. 65:2 I held out my hands all day long to a rebellious people, who walk in a way that is not good, following their own devices. . . .

Phil. 2:8 He humbled himself and became obedient to the point of death—even death on a cross.

Col. 1:15 He is the image of the invisible God, the firstborn of all creation. . . .

Rom. 8:29 For those whom he foreknew he also predestined to be conformed to the image of his Son, in order that he might be the firstborn within a large family.

Question 22. What do you understand by God's providence?

That God not only preserves the world but also continually attends to it, ruling and sustaining it with wise and benevolent care. God is concerned for every creature: "The eyes of all look to you, and you give them their food in due season. You open your hand, you satisfy the desire of every living thing" (Ps. 145:15). In particular, God provides for the world by bringing good out of evil, so that nothing evil is permitted to occur that God does not bend finally to the good. Scripture tells us, for example, how Joseph said to his brothers: "As for you, you meant evil against me; but God meant it for good, to bring it about that many people should be kept alive, as they are today" (Gen. 50:20).

Rom. 8:28 We know that all things work together for good for those who love God, who are called according to his purpose.

Ps. 103:19 The LORD has established his throne in the heavens, and his kingdom rules over all.

Ps. 145:17 The LORD is just in all his ways, and kind in all his doings.

Question 23. What comfort do you receive by trusting in God's providence?

The eternal Father of our Lord Jesus Christ watches over me each day of my life, blessing and guiding me wherever I may be. God strengthens me when I am faithful, comforts me when discouraged or sorrowful, raises me up if I fall, and brings me at last to eternal life. Entrusting myself wholly to God's care, I receive the grace to be patient in adversity, thankful in the midst of blessing, courageous against injustice, and confident that no evil afflicts me that God will not turn to my good.

Ps. 146:9 The LORD watches over the strangers; he upholds the orphan and the widow, but the way of the wicked he brings to ruin.

Isa. 58:11 The LORD will guide you continually, and satisfy your needs in parched places, and make your bones strong; and you shall be like a watered garden, like a spring of water, whose waters never fail.

Isa. 41:10 Do not fear, for I am with you, do not be afraid, for I am your God; I will strengthen you, I will help you, I will uphold you with my victorious right hand.

2 Cor. 1:3–5 Blessed be the God and Father of our Lord Jesus Christ, the Father of mercies and the God of all consolation, who consoles us in all our affliction, so that we may be able to console those who are in any affliction with the consolation with which we ourselves are consoled by God.

Ps. 30:5 For his anger is but for a moment; his favor is for a lifetime. Weeping may linger for the night, but joy comes with the morning.

Question 24. What difference does your faith in God's providence make when you struggle against bitterness and despair?

When I suffer harm or adversity, my faith in God's providence upholds me against bitterness and despair. It reminds me when hope disappears that my heartache and pain are contained by a larger purpose and a higher power than I can presently discern. Even in grief, shame, and loss, I can still cry out to God in lament, waiting on God to supply my needs, and to bring me healing and comfort.

Ps. 42:11 Why are you cast down, O my soul, and why are you disquieted within me? Hope in God; for I shall again praise him, my help and my God.

2 Cor. 4:8–10 We are afflicted in every way, but not crushed; perplexed, but not driven to despair; persecuted, but not forsaken; struck down, but not destroyed; always carrying in the body the death of Jesus, so that the life of Jesus may also be made visible in our bodies.

Ps. 13:1–2 How long, O LORD? Will you forget me forever? How long will you hide your face from me? How long must I bear pain in my soul, and have sorrow in my heart all day long? How long shall my enemy be exalted over me?

Job 7:11 Therefore I will not restrain my mouth; I will speak in the anguish of my spirit; I will complain in the bitterness of my soul.

Question 25. Did God need the world in order to be God?

No. God would still be God, eternally perfect and inexhaustibly rich, even if no creatures had ever been made. Yet without God, all created beings would simply fail to exist. Creatures can neither come into existence, nor continue, nor find fulfillment apart from God. God, however, is self-existent and self-sufficient.

Acts 17:24–25 The God who made the world and everything in it, he who is Lord of heaven and earth, does not live in shrines made by human hands, nor is he served by human hands, as though he needed anything, since he himself gives to all mortals life and breath and all things.

John 1:16 From his fullness we have all received, grace upon grace.

John 5:26 For just as the Father has life in himself, so he has granted the Son also to have life in himself. . . .

Eph. 1:22 And he has put all things under his feet and has made him the head over all things for the church . . .

Question 26. Why then did God create the world?

God's decision to create the world was an act of grace. In this decision God chose to grant existence to the world simply in order to bless it. God created the world to reveal God's glory, to share the love and freedom at the heart of God's triune being, and to give us eternal life in fellowship with God.

Ps. 19:1 The heavens are telling the glory of God; and the firmament proclaims his handiwork.

2 Cor. 3:17 Now the Lord is the Spirit, and where the Spirit of the Lord is, there is freedom.

Ps. 67:6–7 The earth has yielded its increase; God, our God, has blessed us. May God continue to bless us; let all the ends of the earth revere him.

Eph. 1:3–4 Blessed be the God and Father of our Lord Jesus Christ, who has blessed us in Christ with every spiritual blessing in the heavenly places, just as he chose us in Christ before the foundation of the world to be holy and blameless before him in love.

John 3:36 Whoever believes in the Son has eternal life; whoever disobeys the Son will not see life, but must endure God's wrath.

Question 27. Does your confession of God as Creator contradict the findings of modern science?

No. My confession of God as Creator answers three questions: Who?, How?, and Why? It affirms that (a) the triune God, who is self-sufficient, (b) called the world into being out of nothing by the creative power of God's Word (c) for the sake of sharing love and freedom. Natural science has much to teach us about the particular mechanisms and processes of nature, but it is not in a position to answer these questions about ultimate reality, which point to mysteries that science as such is not equipped to explore. Nothing basic to the Christian faith contradicts the findings of modern science, nor does anything essential to modern science contradict the Christian faith.

John 1:1–3 In the beginning was the Word, and the Word was with God, and the Word was God. He was in the beginning with God. All things came into being through him, and without him not one thing came into being.

Question 28. What is the second article of the Apostles' Creed?

"And I believe in Jesus Christ, his only Son, our Lord. He was conceived by the Holy Spirit, born of the Virgin Mary, suffered under Pontius Pilate, was crucified, dead and buried. He descended into hell. On the third day he rose again from the dead. He ascended into heaven and is seated at the right hand of the Father. He will come again to judge the living and the dead."

Question 29. What do you believe when you confess your faith in Jesus Christ as "God's only Son"?

That Jesus Christ is a unique person who was sent to do a unique work.

Luke 3:21–22 Now when all the people were baptized, and when Jesus also had been baptized and was praying, the heaven was opened, and the Holy Spirit descended upon him in bodily form like a dove. And a voice came from heaven, "You are my Son, the Beloved; with you I am well pleased."

Luke 12:49–50 I came to bring fire to the earth, and how I wish it were already kindled! I have a baptism with which to be baptized, and what stress I am under until it is completed!

John 1:14 And the Word became flesh and lived among us, and we have seen his glory, the glory as of a father's only son, full of grace and truth.

Question 30. How do you understand the uniqueness of Jesus Christ?

No one else will ever be God incarnate. No one else will ever die for the sins of the world. Only Jesus Christ is such a person, only he could do such a work, and he in fact has done it.

Isa. 53:5 But he was wounded for our transgressions, crushed for our iniquities; upon him was the punishment that made us whole, and by his bruises we are healed.

John 1:29 The next day he saw Jesus coming toward him and declared, "Here is the Lamb of God who takes away the sin of the world!"

Col. 1:15–20 He is the image of the invisible God, the firstborn of all creation; for in him all things in heaven and on earth were created, things visible and invisible, whether thrones or dominions or rulers or powers—all things have been created through him and for him. He himself is before all things, and in him all things hold together. He is the head of the body, the church; he is the beginning, the firstborn from the dead, so that he might come to have first place in everything. For in him all the fullness of God was pleased to dwell, and through him God was pleased to reconcile to himself all things, whether on earth or in heaven, by making peace through the blood of his cross.

Question 31. What do you affirm when you confess your faith in Jesus Christ as "our Lord"?

That having been raised from the dead he reigns with compassion and justice over all things in heaven and on earth, especially over those who confess him by faith; and that by loving and serving him above all else, I give glory and honor to God.

> *1 Cor. 15:3–4* For I handed on to you as of first importance what I in turn had received: that Christ died for our sins in accordance with the scriptures, and that he was buried, and that he was raised on the third day in accordance with the scriptures. . . .

> *Rev. 11:15* Then the seventh angel blew his trumpet, and there were loud voices in heaven, saying, "The kingdom of the world has become the kingdom of our Lord and of his Messiah, and he will reign forever and ever."

> *Eph. 1:20–2* God put this power to work in Christ when he raised him from the dead and seated him at his right hand in the heavenly places, far above all rule and authority and power and dominion, and above every name that is named, not only in this age but also in the age to come. And he has put all things under his feet and has made him the head over all things for the church, which is his body, the fullness of him who fills all in all.

> *Phil. 2:9–11* Therefore God also highly exalted him and gave him the name that is above every name, so that at the name of Jesus every knee should bend, in heaven and on earth and under the earth, and every tongue should confess that Jesus Christ is Lord, to the glory of God the Father.

Question 32. What do you affirm when you say he was "conceived by the Holy Spirit and born of the Virgin Mary"?

First, that being born of a woman, Jesus was truly a human being. Second, that our Lord's incarnation was a holy and mysterious event, brought about solely by free divine grace surpassing any human possibilities. Third, that from the very beginning of his life on earth, he was set apart by his unique origin for the sake of accomplishing our salvation.

Luke 1:31 And now, you will conceive in your womb and bear a son, and you will name him Jesus.

Luke 1:35 The angel said to her, "The Holy Spirit will come upon you, and the power of the Most High will overshadow you; therefore the child to be born will be holy; he will be called Son of God."

Heb. 2:14 Since, therefore, the children share flesh and blood, he himself likewise shared the same things, so that through death he might destroy the one who has the power of death, that is, the devil. . . .

Phil. 2:5–7 Let the same mind be in you that was in Christ Jesus, who, though he was in the form of God, did not regard equality with God as something to be exploited, but emptied himself, taking the form of a slave, being born in human likeness.

Question 33. What is the significance of affirming that Jesus is truly God?

Only God can properly deserve worship. Only God can reveal to us who God is. And only God can save us from our sins. Being truly God, Jesus meets these conditions. He is the proper object of our worship, the self-revelation of God, and the Savior of the world.

John 20:28 Thomas answered him, "My Lord and my God!" Jesus said to him, "Have you believed because you have seen me? Blessed are those who have not seen and yet have come to believe."

Matt. 11:27 All things have been handed over to me by my Father; and no one knows the Son except the Father, and no one knows the Father except the Son and anyone to whom the Son chooses to reveal him.

1 John 4:14 And we have seen and do testify that the Father has sent his Son as the Savior of the world.

Question 34. What is the significance of affirming that Jesus is also truly a human being?

Being truly human, Jesus entered fully into our fallen situation and overcame it from within. By his pure obedience, he lived a life of unbroken unity with God, even to the point of accepting a violent death. As sinners at war with grace, this is precisely the kind of life we fail to live. When we accept him by faith, he removes our disobedience and clothes us with his perfect righteousness.

Heb. 2:17–18 Therefore he had to become like his brothers and sisters in every respect, so that he might be a merciful and faithful high priest in the service of God, to make a sacrifice of atonement for the sins of the people. Because he himself was tested by what he suffered, he is able to help those who are being tested.

Heb. 4:15 For we do not have a high priest who is unable to sympathize with our weaknesses, but we have one who in every respect has been tested as we are, yet without sin.

Heb. 5:8–9 Although he was a Son, he learned obedience through what he suffered; and having been made perfect, he became the source of eternal salvation for all who obey him. . . .

Rom. 5:19 For just as by the one man's disobedience the many were made sinners, so by the one man's obedience the many will be made righteous.

Question 35. How can Jesus be truly God and yet also truly human at the same time?

The mystery of Jesus Christ's divine-human unity passes our understanding; only faith given by the Holy Spirit enables us to affirm it. When Holy Scripture depicts Jesus as someone with divine power, status, and authority, it presupposes his humanity. And when it depicts him as someone with human weakness, neediness, and mortality, it presupposes his deity.

We cannot understand how this should be, but we can trust that the God who made heaven and earth is free to become God incarnate and thus to be God with us in this wonderful and awe-inspiring way.

Mark 1:27 They were all amazed, and they kept on asking one another, "What is this? A new teaching—with authority! He commands even the unclean spirits, and they obey him."

Mark 4:41 And they were filled with great awe and said to one another, "Who then is this, that even the wind and the sea obey him?"

Matt. 28:18 And Jesus came and said to them, "All authority in heaven and on earth has been given to me."

Luke 22:44 In his anguish he prayed more earnestly, and his sweat became like great drops of blood falling down on the ground.

Job 5:9 He does great things and unsearchable, marvelous things without number.

Question 36. How did God use the people of Israel to prepare the way for the coming of Jesus?

God made a covenant with Israel, promising that God would be their light and their salvation, that they would be God's people, and that through them all the peoples of the earth would be blessed. Therefore, no matter how often Israel turned away from God, God still cared for them and acted on their behalf. In particular, God sent them prophets, priests, and kings. Each of these was "anointed" by God's Spirit—prophets, to declare God's word; priests, to make sacrifice for the people's sins; and kings, to rule justly in the fear of God, upholding the poor and needy, and defending the people from their enemies.

Gen. 17:3–4 Then Abram fell on his face; and God said to him, "As for me, this is my covenant with you: You shall be the ancestor of a multitude of nations."

Gen. 12:1–3 Now the LORD said to Abram, "Go from your country and your kindred and your father's house to the land that I will show you. I will make of you a great nation, and I will bless you, and make your name great, so that you will be a blessing. I will bless those who bless you, and the one who curses you I will curse; and in you all the families of the earth shall be blessed."

Ex. 6:4–5 I also established my covenant with them, to give them the land of Canaan, the land in which they resided as aliens. I have also heard the groaning of the Israelites whom the Egyptians are holding as slaves, and I have remembered my covenant.

Gal. 3:14 . . . in order that in Christ Jesus the blessing of Abraham might come to the Gentiles, so that we might receive the promise of the Spirit through faith.

Jer. 30:22 And you shall be my people, and I will be your God.

1 Peter 2:9–10 But you are a chosen race, a royal priesthood, a holy nation, God's own people, in order that you may proclaim the mighty acts of him who called you out of darkness into his marvelous light. Once you were not a people, but now you are God's people; once you had not received mercy, but now you have received mercy.

Zech. 1:6 But my words and my statutes, which I commanded my servants the prophets, did they not overtake your ancestors? So they repented and said, "The LORD of hosts has dealt with us according to our ways and deeds, just as he planned to do."

Lev. 5:6 And you shall bring to the LORD, as your penalty for the sin that you have committed, . . . a sheep or a goat, as a sin offering; and the priest shall make atonement on your behalf for your sin.

Ps. 72:1, 4 Give your king justice, O God, and your righteousness to a king's son. . . . May he defend the cause of the poor of the people, give deliverance to the needy, and crush the oppressor.

Question 37. Was the covenant with Israel an everlasting covenant?

Yes. With the coming of Jesus the covenant with Israel was expanded and confirmed. By faith in him Gentiles were welcomed into the covenant. This throwing open of the gates confirmed the promise that through Israel God's blessing would come to all peoples. Although for the most part Israel has not accepted Jesus as the Messiah, God has not rejected Israel. God still loves Israel, and God is their hope, "for the gifts and the calling of God are irrevocable" (Rom. 11:29). The God who has reached out to unbelieving Gentiles will not fail to show mercy to Israel as the people of the everlasting covenant.

Isa. 61:8 For I the LORD love justice, I hate robbery and wrongdoing; I will faithfully give them their recompense, and I will make an everlasting covenant with them.

Jer. 31:3 I have loved you with an everlasting love; therefore I have continued my faithfulness to you.

2 Sam. 23:5 Is not my house like this with God? For he has made with me an everlasting covenant, ordered in all things and secure. Will he not cause to prosper all my help and my desire?

Rom. 11:29 For the gifts and the calling of God are irrevocable.

Question 38. Why was the title "Christ," which means "anointed one," applied to Jesus?

Jesus Christ was the definitive prophet, priest, and king. All of the Lord's anointed in Israel anticipated and led finally to him. In assuming these offices Jesus not only transformed them, but also realized the purpose of Israel's election for the sake of the world.

2 Cor. 1:20 For in him every one of God's promises is a "Yes." For this reason it is through him that we say the "Amen," to the glory of God.

Acts 10:37–38 That message spread throughout Judea, beginning in Galilee after the baptism that John announced. . . .

Luke 4:16–19 When he came to Nazareth, where he had been brought up, he went to the synagogue on the sabbath day, as was his custom. He stood up to read, and the scroll of the prophet Isaiah was given to him. He unrolled the scroll and found the place where it was written: "The Spirit of the Lord is upon me, because he has anointed me to bring good news to the poor. He has sent me to proclaim release to the captives and recovery of sight to the blind, to let the oppressed go free, to proclaim the year of the Lord's favor."

Question 39. How did Jesus Christ fulfill the office of prophet?

He was God's Word to a dying and sinful world; he embodied the love he proclaimed. His life, death, and resurrection became the great Yes that continues to be spoken despite how often we have said No. When we receive this Word by faith, Christ himself enters our hearts, that he may dwell in us forever, and we in him.

Acts 3:20, 22 . . . so that times of refreshing may come from the presence of the Lord, and that he may send the Messiah appointed for you, that is, Jesus. . . . Moses said, "The Lord your God will raise up for you from your own people a prophet like me. You must listen to whatever he tells you."

John 1:18 No one has ever seen God. It is God the only Son, who is close to the Father's heart, who has made him known.

Eph. 3:17 . . . and that Christ may dwell in your hearts through faith, as you are being rooted and grounded in love.

Question 40. How did Jesus Christ fulfill the office of priest?

He was the Lamb of God that took away the sin of the world; he became our priest and sacrifice in one. Confronted by our hopelessness in sin and death, Christ interceded by offering himself—his entire person and work—in order to reconcile us to God.

Heb. 4:14 Since, then, we have a great high priest who has passed through the heavens, Jesus, the Son of God, let us hold fast to our confession.

John 1:29 The next day he saw Jesus coming toward him and declared, "Here is the Lamb of God who takes away the sin of the world!"

Heb. 2:17 Therefore he had to become like his brothers and sisters in every respect, so that he might be a merciful and faithful high priest in the service of God, to make a sacrifice of atonement for the sins of the people.

Eph. 1:7 In him we have redemption through his blood, the forgiveness of our trespasses, according to the riches of his grace. . . .

Question 41. How did Jesus Christ fulfill the office of king?

He was the Lord who took the form of a servant; he perfected royal power in weakness. With no sword but the sword of righteousness, and no power but the power of love, Christ defeated sin, evil, and death by reigning from the cross.

John 19:19 Pilate also had an inscription written and put on the cross. It read, "Jesus of Nazareth, the King of the Jews."

Phil. 2:5–8 Let the same mind be in you that was in Christ Jesus, who, though he was in the form of God, did not regard equality with God as something to be exploited, but emptied himself, taking the form of a slave, being born in human likeness. And being found in human form, he humbled himself and became obedient to the point of death—even death on a cross.

1 Cor. 1:25 For God's foolishness is wiser than human wisdom, and God's weakness is stronger than human strength.

John 12:32 And I, when I am lifted up from the earth, will draw all people to myself.

Question 42. What do you affirm when you say that he "suffered under Pontius Pilate"?

First, that our Lord was humiliated, rejected, and abused by the temporal authorities of his day, both religious and political. Christ thus aligned himself with all human beings who are oppressed, tortured, or otherwise shamefully treated by those with worldly power. Second, and even more importantly, that our Lord, though innocent, submitted himself to condemnation by an earthly judge so that through him we ourselves, though guilty, might be acquitted before our heavenly Judge.

Luke 18:32 For he will be handed over to the Gentiles; and he will be mocked and insulted and spat upon.

Isa. 53:3 He was despised and rejected by others; a man of suffering and acquainted with infirmity; and as one from whom others hide their faces he was despised, and we held him of no account.

Ps. 9:9 The LORD is a stronghold for the oppressed, a stronghold in times of trouble.

Luke 1:52 He has brought down the powerful from their thrones, and lifted up the lowly. . . .

2 Cor. 5:21 For our sake he made him to be sin who knew no sin, so that in him we might become the righteousness of God.

2 Tim. 4:8 From now on there is reserved for me the crown of righteousness, which the Lord, the righteous judge, will give me on that day, and not only to me but also to all who have longed for his appearing.

Question 43. What do you affirm when you say that he was "crucified, dead, and buried"?

That when our Lord passed through the door of real human death, he showed us that there is no sorrow he has not known, no grief he has not borne, and no price he was unwilling to pay in order to reconcile us to God.

Matt. 26:38–39 Then he said to them, "I am deeply grieved, even to death; remain here, and stay awake with me." And going a little farther, he threw himself on the ground and prayed, "My Father, if it is possible, let this cup pass from me; yet not what I want but what you want."

Isa. 53:5 But he was wounded for our transgressions, crushed for our iniquities; upon him was the punishment that made us whole, and by his bruises we are healed.

Gal. 3:13 Christ redeemed us from the curse of the law by becoming a curse for us—for it is written, "Cursed is everyone who hangs on a tree. . . ."

Heb. 2:9 But we do see Jesus, who for a little while was made lower than the angels, now crowned with glory and honor because of the suffering of death, so that by the grace of God he might taste death for everyone.

2 Cor. 5:19 In Christ God was reconciling the world to himself, not counting their trespasses against them, and entrusting the message of reconciliation to us.

Question 44. What do you affirm when you say that he "descended into hell"?

That our Lord took upon himself the full consequences of our sinfulness, even the agony of abandonment by God, in order that we might be spared.

Mark 15:34 At three o'clock Jesus cried out with a loud voice, "Eloi, Eloi, lema sabachthani?" which means, "My God, my God, why have you forsaken me?"

Heb. 9:26 . . . for then he would have had to suffer again and again since the foundation of the world. But as it is, he has appeared once for all at the end of the age to remove sin by the sacrifice of himself.

Rom. 4:24–25 It will be reckoned to us who believe in him who raised Jesus our Lord from the dead, who was handed over to death for our trespasses and was raised for our justification.

Question 45. Why did Jesus have to suffer as he did?

Because grace is more abundant—and sin more serious—than we suppose. However cruelly we may treat one another, all sin is primarily against God. God condemns sin, yet never judges apart from grace. In giving Jesus Christ to die for us,

God took the burden of our sin into God's own self to remove it once and for all. The cross in all its severity reveals an abyss of sin swallowed up by the suffering of divine love.

> *Rom. 8:1, 3–4* There is therefore now no condemnation for those who are in Christ Jesus. . . . For God has done what the law, weakened by the flesh, could not do: by sending his own Son in the likeness of sinful flesh, and to deal with sin, he condemned sin in the flesh, so that the just requirement of the law might be fulfilled in us, who walk not according to the flesh but according to the Spirit.
>
> *1 Cor. 1:18* For the message about the cross is foolishness to those who are perishing, but to us who are being saved it is the power of God.
>
> *Rom. 5:8* But God proves his love for us in that while we still were sinners Christ died for us.
>
> *Col. 1:20* And through him God was pleased to reconcile to himself all things, whether on earth or in heaven, by making peace through the blood of his cross.
>
> *James 2:13* For judgment will be without mercy to anyone who has shown no mercy; mercy triumphs over judgment.

Question 46. What do you affirm when you say that "on the third day he rose again from the dead"?

That our Lord could not be held by the power of death. Having died on the cross, he appeared to his followers, triumphant from the grave, in a new, exalted kind of life. In showing them his hands and his feet, the one who was crucified revealed himself to them as the Lord and Savior of the world.

> *Acts 2:24* But God raised him up, having freed him from death, because it was impossible for him to be held in its power.
>
> *1 Cor. 15:3–4* For I handed on to you as of first importance what I in turn had received: that Christ died for our sins in accordance with the scriptures, and that he was buried, and

that he was raised on the third day in accordance with the scriptures. . . .

Luke 24:36–40 While they were talking about this, Jesus himself stood among them and said to them, "Peace be with you." They were startled and terrified, and thought that they were seeing a ghost. He said to them, "Why are you frightened, and why do doubts arise in your hearts? Look at my hands and my feet; see that it is I myself. Touch me and see; for a ghost does not have flesh and bones as you see that I have." And when he had said this, he showed them his hands and his feet.

John 20:15–18 Jesus said to her, "Woman, why are you weeping? Whom are you looking for?" Supposing him to be the gardener, she said to him, "Sir, if you have carried him away, tell me where you have laid him, and I will take him away." Jesus said to her, "Mary!" She turned and said to him in Hebrew, "Rabbouni!" (which means Teacher). Jesus said to her, "Do not hold on to me, because I have not yet ascended to the Father. But go to my brothers and say to them, 'I am ascending to my Father and your Father, to my God and your God.'" Mary Magdalene went and announced to the disciples, "I have seen the Lord"; and she told them that he had said these things to her.

1 Cor. 15:5–8 . . . and that he appeared to Cephas, then to the twelve. Then he appeared to more than five hundred brothers and sisters at one time, most of whom are still alive, though some have died. Then he appeared to James, then to all the apostles. Last of all, as to one untimely born, he appeared also to me.

John 20:27 Then he said to Thomas, "Put your finger here and see my hands. Reach out your hand and put it in my side. Do not doubt but believe."

Question 47. What do you affirm when you say that "he ascended into heaven and is seated at the right hand of the Father"?

First, that Christ has gone to be with the Father, hidden except to the eyes of faith. Second, however, that Christ is not cut off from us in the remote past, or in some place from which he cannot reach us, but is present to us here and now by grace. He reigns with divine authority, protecting us, guiding us, and interceding for us until he returns in glory.

Acts 1:6–11 So when they had come together, they asked him, "Lord, is this the time when you will restore the kingdom to Israel?" He replied, "It is not for you to know the times or periods that the Father has set by his own authority. But you will receive power when the Holy Spirit has come upon you; and you will be my witnesses in Jerusalem, in all Judea and Samaria, and to the ends of the earth." When he had said this, as they were watching, he was lifted up, and a cloud took him out of their sight. While he was going and they were gazing up toward heaven, suddenly two men in white robes stood by them. They said, "Men of Galilee, why do you stand looking up toward heaven? This Jesus, who has been taken up from you into heaven, will come in the same way as you saw him go into heaven."

Col. 3:1 So if you have been raised with Christ, seek the things that are above, where Christ is, seated at the right hand of God.

Question 48. How do you understand the words that "he will come again to judge the living and the dead"?

Like everyone else, I too must stand in fear and trembling before the judgment seat of Christ. But the Judge is the one who submitted to judgment for my sake. Nothing will be able to separate me from the love of God in Christ Jesus my Lord. All the sinful failures that cause me shame will perish as through fire, while any good I may have done will be received with gladness by God.

2 Cor. 5:10 For all of us must appear before the judgment seat of Christ, so that each may receive recompense for what has been done in the body, whether good or evil.

Eccl. 12:14 For God will bring every deed into judgment, including every secret thing, whether good or evil.

Acts 17:31 He has fixed a day on which he will have the world judged in righteousness by a man whom he has appointed, and of this he has given assurance to all by raising him from the dead.

Rom. 8:38–39 For I am convinced that neither death, nor life, nor angels, nor rulers, nor things present, nor things to come, nor powers, nor height, nor depth, nor anything else in all creation, will be able to separate us from the love of God in Christ Jesus our Lord.

1 John 4:17 Love has been perfected among us in this: that we may have boldness on the day of judgment, because as he is, so are we in this world.

1 Cor. 3:12–15 Now if anyone builds on the foundation with gold, silver, precious stones, wood, hay, straw—the work of each builder will become visible, for the Day will disclose it, because it will be revealed with fire, and the fire will test what sort of work each has done. If what has been built on the foundation survives, the builder will receive a reward. If the work is burned up, the builder will suffer loss; the builder will be saved, but only as through fire.

Acts 10:42 He commanded us to preach to the people and to testify that he is the one ordained by God as judge of the living and the dead.

Question 49. Will all human beings be saved?

No one will be lost who can be saved. The limits to salvation, whatever they may be, are known only to God. Three truths above all are certain. God is a holy God who is not to be trifled with. No one will be saved except by grace alone. And no judge could possibly be more gracious than our Lord and Savior, Jesus Christ.

Heb. 10:31 It is a fearful thing to fall into the hands of the living God.

Rom. 11:32 For God has imprisoned all in disobedience so that he may be merciful to all.

Luke 15:4–7 Which one of you, having a hundred sheep and losing one of them, does not leave the ninety-nine in the wilderness and go after the one that is lost until he finds it? When he has found it, he lays it on his shoulders and rejoices. And when he comes home, he calls together his friends and neighbors, saying to them, "Rejoice with me, for I have found my sheep that was lost." Just so, I tell you, there will be more joy in heaven over one sinner who repents than over ninety-nine righteous persons who need no repentance.

Eph. 2:8 For by grace you have been saved through faith, and this is not your own doing; it is the gift of God. . . .

1 Tim. 2:3–4 This is right and is acceptable in the sight of God our Savior, who desires everyone to be saved and to come to the knowledge of the truth.

John 3:17–18 Indeed, God did not send the Son into the world to condemn the world, but in order that the world might be saved through him. Those who believe in him are not condemned; but those who do not believe are condemned already, because they have not believed in the name of the only Son of God.

Ezek. 18:32 For I have no pleasure in the death of anyone, says the Lord GOD. Turn, then, and live.

2 Cor. 5:14–15 For the love of Christ urges us on, because we are convinced that one has died for all; therefore all have died. And he died for all, so that those who live might live no longer for themselves, but for him who died and was raised for them.

Question 50. Is Christianity the only true religion?

Religion is a complex matter. When used as a means to promote self-justification, war-mongering, or prejudice, it is a form of sin. Too often all religions—and not least Christianity—have been twisted in this way. Nevertheless, by grace, despite all disobedience, Christianity offers the truth of the gospel. Although other religions may enshrine various truths, no other can or does affirm the name of Jesus Christ as the hope of the world.

Matt 7:3 Why do you see the speck in your neighbor's eye, but do not notice the log in your own eye?

James 1:26 If any think they are religious, and do not bridle their tongues but deceive their hearts, their religion is worthless.

James 1:27 Religion that is pure and undefiled before God, the Father, is this: to care for orphans and widows in their distress, and to keep oneself unstained by the world.

Acts 4:12 There is salvation in no one else, for there is no other name under heaven given among mortals by which we must be saved.

John 14:6 Jesus said to him, "I am the way, and the truth, and the life. No one comes to the Father except through me."

Rom. 1:16 For I am not ashamed of the gospel; it is the power of God for salvation to everyone who has faith, to the Jew first and also to the Greek.

2 Cor. 4:7 But we have this treasure in clay jars, so that it may be made clear that this extraordinary power belongs to God and does not come from us.

Question 51. How will God deal with the followers of other religions?

God has made salvation available to all human beings through Jesus Christ, crucified and risen. How God will deal with those who do not know or follow Christ, but who follow another tradition, we cannot finally say. We can say, however, that God is gracious and merciful, and that God will not deal with people in any other way than we see in Jesus Christ, who came as the Savior of the world.

Rev. 7:9 After this I looked, and there was a great multitude that no one could count, from every nation, from all tribes and peoples and languages, standing before the throne and before the Lamb, robed in white, with palm branches in their hands.

Ps. 103:8 The LORD is merciful and gracious, slow to anger and abounding in steadfast love.

John 3:19 And this is the judgment, that the light has come into the world, and people loved darkness rather than light because their deeds were evil.

Titus 2:11 For the grace of God has appeared, bringing salvation to all. . . .

Question 52. How should I treat non-Christians and people of other religions?

As much as I can, I should meet friendship with friendship, hostility with kindness, generosity with gratitude, persecution with forbearance, truth with agreement, and error with truth. I should express my faith with humility and devotion as the occasion requires, whether silently or openly, boldly or meekly, by word or by deed. I should avoid compromising the truth on the one hand and being narrow-minded on the other. In short, I should always welcome and accept these others in a way that honors and reflects the Lord's welcome and acceptance of me.

Rom. 15:7 Welcome one another, therefore, just as Christ has welcomed you, for the glory of God.

Luke 6:37 Do not judge, and you will not be judged; do not condemn, and you will not be condemned. Forgive, and you will be forgiven.

Matt. 5:44 But I say to you, Love your enemies and pray for those who persecute you. . . .

Eph. 4:25 So then, putting away falsehood, let all of us speak the truth to our neighbors, for we are members of one another.

Acts. 13:47 For so the Lord has commanded us, saying, "I have set you to be a light for the Gentiles, so that you may bring salvation to the ends of the earth."

Rom. 12:21 Do not be overcome by evil, but overcome evil with good.

Rom. 13:10 Love does no wrong to a neighbor; therefore, love is the fulfilling of the law.

Question 53. What is the third article of the Apostles' Creed?

"I believe in the Holy Spirit, the holy catholic church, the communion of saints, the forgiveness of sins, the resurrection of the body, and the life everlasting. Amen."

Question 54. What do you believe when you confess your faith in the Holy Spirit?

Apart from the Holy Spirit, our Lord can neither be loved, nor known, nor served. The Holy Spirit is the personal bond by which Jesus Christ unites us to himself, the teacher who opens our hearts to Christ, and the comforter who leads us to repentance, empowering us to live in Christ's service. As the work of the one Holy Spirit, our love, knowledge, and service of Christ are all inseparably related.

John 14:26 But the Advocate, the Holy Spirit, whom the Father will send in my name, will teach you everything, and remind you of all that I have said to you.

1 Cor. 12:3 Therefore I want you to understand that no one speaking by the Spirit of God ever says "Let Jesus be cursed!" and no one can say "Jesus is Lord" except by the Holy Spirit.

Rom. 5:5 And hope does not disappoint us, because God's love has been poured into our hearts through the Holy Spirit that has been given to us.

1 Cor. 6:17, 19 But anyone united to the Lord becomes one spirit with him. . . . Or do you not know that your body is a temple of the Holy Spirit within you, which you have from God, and that you are not your own?

1 Cor. 3:16 Do you not know that you are God's temple and that God's Spirit dwells in you?

John 4:24 God is spirit, and those who worship him must worship in spirit and truth.

Question 55. How do we receive the Holy Spirit?

By receiving the Word of God. As the midwife of the new creation, the Spirit arrives with the Word, brings us to rebirth, and assures us of eternal life. The Spirit nurtures, corrects, and strengthens us with the pure spiritual milk of the Word (1 Peter 2:2).

Eph. 6:17 Take the helmet of salvation, and the sword of the Spirit, which is the word of God.

John 14:16–17 And I will ask the Father, and he will give you another Advocate, to be with you forever. This is the Spirit of truth, whom the world cannot receive, because it neither sees him nor knows him. You know him, because he abides with you, and he will be in you.

John 3:5–6 Jesus answered, "Very truly, I tell you, no one can enter the kingdom of God without being born of water and Spirit. What is born of the flesh is flesh, and what is born of the Spirit is spirit."

Luke 11:13 If you then, who are evil, know how to give good gifts to your children, how much more will the heavenly Father give the Holy Spirit to those who ask him!

1 Thess. 1:5 . . . because our message of the gospel came to you not in word only, but also in power and in the Holy Spirit and with full conviction; just as you know what kind of persons we proved to be among you for your sake.

John 16:8 When he comes, he will prove the world wrong about sin and righteousness and judgment. . . .

Rom. 8:15–16 For you did not receive a spirit of slavery to fall back into fear, but you have received a spirit of adoption. When we cry, "Abba! Father!" it is that very Spirit bearing witness with our spirit that we are children of God . . .

1 Peter 2:2 Like newborn infants, long for the pure, spiritual milk, so that by it you may grow into salvation. . . .

Question 56. What do you mean when you speak of "the Word of God"?

"Jesus Christ, as he is attested for us in Holy Scripture, is the one Word of God which we have to hear and which we have to trust and obey in life and in death" (Barmen Declaration, Article I).

John 1:1–5 In the beginning was the Word, and the Word was with God, and the Word was God. He was in the beginning with God. All things came into being through him, and without him not one thing came into being. What has come into being in him was life, and the life was the light of all people. The light shines in the darkness, and the darkness did not overcome it.

John 1:14 And the Word became flesh and lived among us, and we have seen his glory, the glory as of a father's only son, full of grace and truth.

Question 57. Isn't Holy Scripture also the Word of God?

Yes. Holy Scripture is also God's Word because of its content, its function, and its origin. Its central content is Jesus Christ, the living Word. Its basic function is to deepen our love, knowledge, and service of him as our Savior and Lord. And its ultimate origin is in the Holy Spirit, who spoke through the prophets and apostles, and who inspires us with eager desire for the truths that Scripture contains.

2 Tim. 3:16 All scripture is inspired by God and is useful for teaching, for reproof, for correction, and for training in righteousness. . . .

John 5:39 You search the scriptures because you think that in them you have eternal life; and it is they that testify on my behalf.

Question 58. Isn't preaching also the Word of God?

Yes. Preaching and other forms of Christian witness are also God's Word when they are faithful to the witness of Holy Scripture. By the power of the Spirit, preaching actually gives to us what it proclaims—the real presence of our Lord Jesus Christ. Faith comes by hearing God's Word in the form of faithful proclamation.

Mark 16:15 And he said to them, "Go into all the world and proclaim the good news to the whole creation."

2 Cor. 4:5 For we do not proclaim ourselves; we proclaim Jesus Christ as Lord and ourselves as your slaves for Jesus' sake.

Rom. 1:15–16 . . . hence my eagerness to proclaim the gospel to you also who are in Rome. For I am not ashamed of the gospel; it is the power of God for salvation to everyone who has faith, to the Jew first and also to the Greek.

Rom. 10:17 So faith comes from what is heard, and what is heard comes through the word of Christ.

Question 59. Does the Holy Spirit ever speak apart from God's Word in its written and proclaimed forms?

Since the Spirit is not given to the church without the Word, true proclamation depends on Scripture. Since the Word cannot be grasped without the Spirit, true interpretation depends on prayer. However, as the wind blows where it will, so may the Spirit speak or work in people's lives in unexpected or indirect ways, yet always according to the Word, never contradicting or diluting it.

John 3:8 The wind blows where it chooses, and you hear the sound of it, but you do not know where it comes from or where it goes. So it is with everyone who is born of the Spirit.

Acts 8:29–31 Then the Spirit said to Philip, "Go over to this chariot and join it." So Philip ran up to it and heard him reading the prophet Isaiah. He asked, "Do you understand what you are reading?" He replied, "How can I, unless someone guides me?" And he invited Philip to get in and sit beside him.

Eph. 6:18 Pray in the Spirit at all times in every prayer and supplication. To that end keep alert and always persevere in supplication for all the saints.

2 Peter 1:20–21 First of all you must understand this, that no prophecy of scripture is a matter of one's own interpretation, because no prophecy ever came by human will, but men and women moved by the Holy Spirit spoke from God.

Question 60. Aren't people without faith sometimes wiser than those who have faith?

Yes. The important question for the church is not so much where an insight may come from as the norm by which to test it. Truth is where one finds it, whether inside or outside the church, and whether supporting or contradicting one's own most cherished opinions. Our faithful discernment of what is true, however, depends finally on God's Word as conveyed in Holy Scripture. The church is therefore reformed and always being reformed according to the Word of God.

Titus 1:9 He must have a firm grasp of the word that is trustworthy in accordance with the teaching, so that he may be able both to preach with sound doctrine and to refute those who contradict it.

Luke 16:8b For the children of this age are more shrewd in dealing with their own generation than are the children of light.

Isa. 45:4 For the sake of my servant Jacob, and Israel my chosen, I call you by your name, I surname you, though you do not know me.

Num. 22:28 Then the Lord opened the mouth of the donkey, and it said to Balaam, "What have I done to you, that you have struck me these three times?"

Question 61. Doesn't modern critical scholarship undermine your belief that Holy Scripture is a form of God's Word?

No. The methods of modern scholarship are a good servant but a bad master. They are neither to be accepted nor rejected uncritically. Properly used they help us rightly and richly interpret Scripture; improperly used they can usurp the place of faith (or establish an alternative faith). Wise interpreters use these methods in the service of faithful witness and understanding. The methods of modern scholarship remain a useful tool, while Holy Scripture remains reliable in all essential matters of faith and practice.

Prov. 1:5–6 Let the wise also hear and gain in learning, and the discerning acquire skill, to understand a proverb and a figure, the words of the wise and their riddles.

Prov. 10:14 The wise lay up knowledge, but the babbling of a fool brings ruin near.

1 Cor. 1:20, 25 Where is the one who is wise? Where is the scribe? Where is the debater of this age? Has not God made foolish the wisdom of the world? . . . For God's foolishness is wiser than human wisdom, and God's weakness is stronger than human strength.

Question 62. What do you affirm when you speak of "the holy catholic church"?

The church is the company of all faithful people who have given their lives to Jesus Christ, as he has given and gives himself to them. Since Christ cannot be separated from his people, the church is holy because he is holy, and universal (or "catholic") in significance because he is universal in significance. Despite all its remaining imperfections here and now, the church is called to become ever more holy and catholic, for that is what it already is in Christ.

Gal. 2:20 It is no longer I who live, but it is Christ who lives in me. And the life I now live in the flesh I live by faith in the Son of God, who loved me and gave himself for me.

1 Cor. 1:2 To the church of God that is in Corinth, to those who are sanctified in Christ Jesus, called to be saints, together with all those who in every place call on the name of our Lord Jesus Christ, both their Lord and ours . . .

Lev. 11:44 For I am the LORD your God; sanctify yourselves therefore, and be holy, for I am holy.

1 Peter 1:15–16 Instead, as he who called you is holy, be holy yourselves in all your conduct; for it is written, "You shall be holy, for I am holy."

Rev. 5:9 They sing a new song: "You are worthy to take the scroll and to open its seals, for you were slaughtered and by your blood you ransomed for God saints from every tribe and language and people and nation. . . ."

Question 63. What is the mission of the church?

The mission of the church is to bear witness to God's love for the world in Jesus Christ.

Acts 1:8 But you will receive power when the Holy Spirit has come upon you; and you will be my witnesses in Jerusalem, in all Judea and Samaria, and to the ends of the earth.

John 15:26–27 When the Advocate comes, whom I will send to you from the Father, the Spirit of truth who comes from the Father, he will testify on my behalf. You also are to testify because you have been with me from the beginning.

Eph. 3:8–10 Although I am the very least of all the saints, this grace was given to me to bring to the Gentiles the news of the boundless riches of Christ, and to make everyone see what is the plan of the mystery hidden for ages in God who created all things; so that through the church the wisdom of God in its rich variety might now be made known to the rulers and authorities in the heavenly places.

Question 64. What forms does this mission take?

The forms are as various as the forms of God's love, yet the center is always Jesus Christ. The church is faithful to its mission when it extends mercy and forgiveness to the needy in ways that point finally to him. For in the end it is always by Christ's mercy that the needs of the needy are met.

Luke 10:37 He said, "The one who showed him mercy." Jesus said to him, "Go and do likewise."

Eph. 4:32 Be kind to one another, tenderhearted, forgiving one another, as God in Christ has forgiven you.

Deut. 15:11 Since there will never cease to be some in need on the earth, I therefore command you, "Open your hand to the poor and needy neighbor in your land."

Acts 4:34 There was not a needy person among them, for as many as owned lands or houses sold them and brought the proceeds of what was sold.

Question 65. Who are the needy?

The hungry need bread, the homeless need a roof, the oppressed need justice, and the lonely need fellowship. At the same time—on another and deeper level—the hopeless need hope, sinners need forgiveness, and the world needs the gospel. On this level no one is excluded, and all the needy are one. Our mission as the church is to bring hope to a desperate world by declaring God's undying love—as one beggar tells another where to find bread.

Ps. 10:12 Rise up, O LORD; O God, lift up your hand; do not forget the oppressed.

Matt. 25:37–40 Then the righteous will answer him, "Lord, when was it that we saw you hungry and gave you food, or thirsty and gave you something to drink? And when was it that we saw you a stranger and welcomed you, or naked and gave you clothing? And when was it that we saw you sick or in prison and visited you?" And the king will answer them, "Truly I tell you, just as you did it to one of the least of these who are members of my family, you did it to me."

Jer. 9:23 Thus says the LORD: Do not let the wise boast in their wisdom, do not let the mighty boast in their might, do not let the wealthy boast in their wealth. . . .

1 Cor. 9:16 If I proclaim the gospel, this gives me no ground for boasting, for an obligation is laid on me, and woe to me if I do not proclaim the gospel!

Eph. 6:19 Pray also for me, so that when I speak, a message may be given to me to make known with boldness the mystery of the gospel. . . .

Question 66. What do you affirm when you speak of "the communion of saints"?

All those who live in union with Christ, whether on earth or with God in heaven, are "saints." Our communion with Christ makes us members one of another. As by his death he removed our separation from God, so by his Spirit he removes all that divides us from each other. Breaking down every wall of hostility, he makes us, who are many, one body in himself. The ties that bind us in Christ are deeper than any other human relationship.

Eph. 2:19–20 So then you are no longer strangers and aliens, but you are citizens with the saints and also members of the household of God, built upon the foundation of the apostles and prophets, with Christ Jesus himself as the cornerstone.

Rom. 12:5 . . . so we, who are many, are one body in Christ, and individually we are members one of another.

Eph. 2:14 For he is our peace; in his flesh he has made both groups into one and has broken down the dividing wall, that is, the hostility between us.

1 Cor. 12:27 Now you are the body of Christ and individually members of it.

Gal. 3:28 There is no longer Jew or Greek, there is no longer slave or free, there is no longer male and female; for all of you are one in Christ Jesus.

Eph. 4:4 There is one body and one Spirit, just as you were called to the one hope of your calling. . . .

1 Cor. 12:4–7, 12–13 Now there are varieties of gifts, but the same Spirit; and there are varieties of services, but the same Lord; and there are varieties of activities, but it is the same God who activates all of them in everyone. To each is given the manifestation of the Spirit for the common good. . . . For just as the body is one and has many members, and all the members of the body, though many, are one body, so it is with Christ. For in the one Spirit we were all baptized into one body—Jews or Greeks, slaves or free—and we were all made to drink of one Spirit.

Question 67. How do you enter into communion with Christ and so with one another?

By the power of the Holy Spirit as it works through Word and Sacrament. Because the Spirit uses them for our salvation, Word and Sacrament are called "means of grace." The Scriptures acknowledge two sacraments as instituted by our Lord Jesus Christ—baptism and the Lord's Supper.

> *1 Cor. 10:17* Because there is one bread, we who are many are one body, for we all partake of the one bread.

> *1 Cor. 12:13* For in the one Spirit we were all baptized into one body—Jews or Greeks, slaves or free—and we were all made to drink of one Spirit.

> *Col. 3:16* Let the word of Christ dwell in you richly; teach and admonish one another in all wisdom; and with gratitude in your hearts sing psalms, hymns, and spiritual songs to God.

Question 68. What is a sacrament?

A sacrament is a special act of Christian worship, instituted by Christ, which uses a visible sign to proclaim the promise of the gospel for the forgiveness of sins and eternal life. The sacramental sign seals this promise to believers by grace and brings to them what is promised. In baptism the sign is that of water; in the Lord's Supper, that of bread and wine.

> *Mark 1:9–11* In those days Jesus came from Nazareth of Galilee and was baptized by John in the Jordan. And just as he was coming up out of the water, he saw the heavens torn apart and the Spirit descending like a dove on him. And a voice came from heaven, "You are my Son, the Beloved; with you I am well pleased."

> *Mark 14:22–25* While they were eating, he took a loaf of bread, and after blessing it he broke it, gave it to them, and said, "Take; this is my body." Then he took a cup, and after giving thanks he gave it to them, and all of them drank from it. He said to them, "This is my blood of the covenant, which is poured out for many. Truly I tell you, I will never again drink of the fruit of the vine until that day when I drink it new in the kingdom of God."

Question 69. How do you understand the relationship between the word of promise and the sacramental sign?

Take away the word of promise, and the water is merely water, or the bread and wine, merely bread and wine. But add water, or bread and wine, to the word of promise, and it becomes a visible word. In this form it does what by grace the word always does: it brings the salvation it promises, and conveys to faith the real presence of our Lord Jesus Christ. The sacraments are visible words which uniquely assure and confirm that no matter how greatly I may have sinned, Christ died also for me, and comes to live in me and with me.

Luke 24:30–31 When he was at the table with them, he took bread, blessed and broke it, and gave it to them. Then their eyes were opened, and they recognized him; and he vanished from their sight.

1 Cor. 10:16 The cup of blessing that we bless, is it not a sharing in the blood of Christ? The bread that we break, is it not a sharing in the body of Christ?

Matt. 28:20 . . . teaching them to obey everything that I have commanded you. And remember, I am with you always, to the end of the age.

Col. 1:27 To them God chose to make known how great among the Gentiles are the riches of the glory of this mystery, which is Christ in you, the hope of glory.

Question 70. What is the main difference between baptism and the Lord's Supper?

While I receive baptism only once, I receive the Lord's Supper again and again. Being unrepeatable, baptism indicates not only that Christ died for our sins once and for all, but that by grace we are also united with him once and for all through faith. Being repeatable, the Lord's Supper indicates that as we turn unfilled to him again and again, our Lord continually meets us in the power of the Holy Spirit to renew and deepen our faith.

Acts 2:41 So those who welcomed his message were baptized, and that day about three thousand persons were added.

John 6:33 For the bread of God is that which comes down from heaven and gives life to the world.

John 6:51 I am the living bread that came down from heaven. Whoever eats of this bread will live forever; and the bread that I will give for the life of the world is my flesh.

John 6:56 Those who eat my flesh and drink my blood abide in me, and I in them.

1 Cor. 11:26 For as often as you eat this bread and drink the cup, you proclaim the Lord's death until he comes.

Question 71. What is baptism?

Baptism is the sign and seal through which we are joined to Christ.

Rom. 6:3–4 Do you not know that all of us who have been baptized into Christ Jesus were baptized into his death? Therefore we have been buried with him by baptism into death, so that, just as Christ was raised from the dead by the glory of the Father, so we too might walk in newness of life.

Gal. 3:27 As many of you as were baptized into Christ have clothed yourselves with Christ.

Rom. 4:11 He received the sign of circumcision as a seal of the righteousness that he had by faith when he was still uncircumcised. The purpose was to make him the ancestor of all who believe without being circumcised and who thus have righteousness reckoned to them. . . .

Question 72. What does it mean to be baptized?

My baptism means that I am joined to Jesus Christ forever. I am baptized into his death and resurrection, along with all who have received him by faith. As I am baptized with water, he baptizes me with his Spirit, washing away all my sins and freeing me from their control. My baptism is a sign that one day I will rise with him in glory, and may walk with him even now in newness of life.

Col. 2:12 . . . When you were buried with him in baptism, you were also raised with him through faith in the power of God, who raised him from the dead.

Mark 1:8 I have baptized you with water; but he will baptize you with the Holy Spirit.

1 Cor. 6:11 And this is what some of you used to be. But you were washed, you were sanctified, you were justified in the name of the Lord Jesus Christ and in the Spirit of our God.

Eph. 4:4–6 There is one body and one Spirit, just as you were called to the one hope of your calling, one Lord, one faith, one baptism, one God and Father of all, who is above all and through all and in all.

Question 73. Are infants also to be baptized?

Yes. Along with their believing parents, they are included in the great hope of the gospel and belong to the people of God. Forgiveness and faith are both promised to them as gifts through Christ's covenant with his people. These children are therefore to be received into the community by baptism, nurtured in the Word of God, and confirmed at an appropriate time by their own profession of faith.

Gen. 17:7 I will establish my covenant between me and you, and your offspring after you throughout their generations, for an everlasting covenant, to be God to you and to your offspring after you.

Acts 2:38–39 Peter said to them, "Repent, and be baptized every one of you in the name of Jesus Christ so that your sins may be forgiven; and you will receive the gift of the Holy Spirit. For the promise is for you, for your children, and for all who are far away, everyone whom the Lord our God calls to him."

Acts 16:15 When she and her household were baptized, she urged us, saying, "If you have judged me to be faithful to the Lord, come and stay at my home." And she prevailed upon us.

Acts 16:33 At the same hour of the night he took them and washed their wounds; then he and his entire family were baptized without delay.

Acts 18:8 Crispus, the official of the synagogue, became a believer in the Lord, together with all his household; and many of the Corinthians who heard Paul became believers and were baptized.

Question 74. Should infants be baptized if their parents or guardians have no relation to the church?

No. It would be irresponsible to baptize an infant without at least one Christian parent or guardian who promises to nurture the infant in the life of the community and to instruct it in the Christian faith.

Eph. 6:4 And, fathers, do not provoke your children to anger, but bring them up in the discipline and instruction of the Lord.

2 Tim. 1:5 I am reminded of your sincere faith, a faith that lived first in your grandmother Lois and your mother Eunice and now, I am sure, lives in you.

1 Cor. 7:14 For the unbelieving husband is made holy through his wife, and the unbelieving wife is made holy through her husband. Otherwise, your children would be unclean, but as it is, they are holy.

Question 75. In what name are you baptized?

In the name of the Trinity. After he was raised from the dead, our Lord appeared to his disciples and said to them, "Go therefore and make disciples of all nations, baptizing them in the name of the Father and of the Son and of the Holy Spirit" (Matt. 28:19).

Matt. 28:16–20 Now the eleven disciples went to Galilee, to the mountain to which Jesus had directed them. When they saw him, they worshiped him; but some doubted. And Jesus came and said to them, "All authority in heaven and on earth has been given to me. Go therefore and make disciples of all nations, baptizing them in the name of the Father and of the Son and of the Holy Spirit, and teaching them to obey everything that I have commanded you. And remember, I am with you always, to the end of the age."

Matt. 3:16–17 And when Jesus had been baptized, just as he came up from the water, suddenly the heavens were opened to him and he saw the Spirit of God descending like a dove and alighting on him. And a voice from heaven said, "This is my Son, the Beloved, with whom I am well pleased."

1 Peter 1:2 [To those] who have been chosen and destined by God the Father and sanctified by the Spirit to be obedient to Jesus Christ and to be sprinkled with his blood: May grace and peace be yours in abundance.

1 Cor. 12:4–6 Now there are varieties of gifts, but the same Spirit; and there are varieties of services, but the same Lord; and there are varieties of activities, but it is the same God who activates all of them in everyone.

Question 76. What is the meaning of this name?

It is the name of the Holy Trinity. The Father is God, the Son is God, and the Holy Spirit is God. And yet they are not three gods, but one God in three persons. We worship God in this mystery.

2 Cor. 13:13 The grace of the Lord Jesus Christ, the love of God, and the communion of the Holy Spirit be with all of you.

John 1:1–4 In the beginning was the Word, and the Word was with God, and the Word was God. He was in the beginning with God. All things came into being through him, and without him not one thing came into being. What has come into being in him was life, and the life was the light of all people.

Rom. 8:11 If the Spirit of him who raised Jesus from the dead dwells in you, he who raised Christ from the dead will give life to your mortal bodies also through his Spirit that dwells in you.

John 16:13–15 When the Spirit of truth comes, he will guide you into all the truth; for he will not speak on his own, but will speak whatever he hears, and he will declare to you the things that are to come. He will glorify me, because he will take what is mine and declare it to you. All that the Father has is mine. For this reason I said that he will take what is mine and declare it to you.

Question 77. What is the Lord's Supper?

The Lord's Supper is the sign and seal by which our communion with Christ is renewed.

1 Cor. 10:16 The cup of blessing that we bless, is it not a sharing in the blood of Christ? The bread that we break, is it not a sharing in the body of Christ?

Question 78. What does it mean to share in the Lord's Supper?

When we celebrate the Lord's Supper, the Lord Jesus Christ is truly present, pouring out his Spirit upon us. By his Spirit, the bread that we break and the cup that we bless share in our Lord's own body and blood. Through them he once offered our life to God; through them he now offers his life to us. As I receive the bread and the cup, remembering that Christ died even for me, I feed on him in my heart by faith with thanksgiving, and enter his risen life, so that his life becomes mine, and my life becomes his, to all eternity.

1 Cor. 11:23–26 For I received from the Lord what I also handed on to you, that the Lord Jesus on the night when he was betrayed took a loaf of bread, and when he had given thanks, he broke it and said, "This is my body that is for you. Do this in remembrance of me." In the same way he took the cup also, after supper, saying, "This cup is the new covenant in my blood. Do this, as often as you drink it, in remembrance of me." For as often as you eat this bread and drink the cup, you proclaim the Lord's death until he comes.

Mark 14:22–25 While they were eating, he took a loaf of bread, and after blessing it he broke it, gave it to them, and said, "Take; this is my body." Then he took a cup, and after giving thanks he gave it to them, and all of them drank from it. He said to them, "This is my blood of the covenant, which is poured out for many. Truly I tell you, I will never again drink of the fruit of the vine until that day when I drink it new in the kingdom of God."

Question 79. Who may receive the Lord's Supper?

All baptized Christians who rejoice in so great a gift, who confess their sins, and who draw near with faith intending to lead a new life, may receive the Lord's Supper. This includes baptized children who have expressed a desire to participate and who have been instructed in the meaning of the sacrament in a way they can understand.

Luke 13:29 Then people will come from east and west, from north and south, and will eat in the kingdom of God.

1 Cor. 11:28 Examine yourselves, and only then eat of the bread and drink of the cup.

Phil. 4:4 Rejoice in the Lord always; again I will say, Rejoice.

Question 80. What do you mean when you speak of "the forgiveness of sins"?

That because of Jesus Christ, God no longer holds my sins against me. Christ alone is my righteousness and my life; Christ is my only hope. Grace alone, not my merits, is the basis on which God has forgiven me in him. Faith alone, not my works, is the means by which I receive Christ into my heart, and with him the forgiveness that makes me whole. Christ alone, grace alone, and faith alone bring the forgiveness I receive through the gospel.

1 Cor. 1:30 He is the source of your life in Christ Jesus, who became for us wisdom from God, and righteousness and sanctification and redemption. . . .

1 Tim. 1:1 Paul, an apostle of Christ Jesus by the command of God our Savior and of Christ Jesus our hope. . . .

Rom. 11:6 But if it is by grace, it is no longer on the basis of works, otherwise grace would no longer be grace.

Eph. 2:8 For by grace you have been saved through faith, and this is not your own doing; it is the gift of God. . . .

Rom. 5:15 But the free gift is not like the trespass. For if the many died through the one man's trespass, much more surely have the grace of God and the free gift in the grace of the one man, Jesus Christ, abounded for the many.

Rom. 4:16 For this reason it depends on faith, in order that the promise may rest on grace and be guaranteed to all his descendants, not only to the adherents of the law but also to those who share the faith of Abraham (for he is the father of all of us). . . .

Rom. 3:28 For we hold that a person is justified by faith apart from works prescribed by the law.

Question 81. Does forgiveness mean that God condones sin?

No. God does not cease to be God. Although God is merciful, God does not condone what God forgives. In the death and resurrection of Christ, God judges what God abhors—everything hostile to love—by abolishing it at the very roots. In this judgment the unexpected occurs: good is brought out of evil, hope out of hopelessness, and life out of death. God spares sinners and turns them from enemies into friends. The uncompromising judgment of God is revealed in the suffering love of the cross.

Hab. 1:13 Your eyes are too pure to behold evil, and you cannot look on wrongdoing; why do you look on the treacherous, and are silent when the wicked swallow those more righteous than they?

Isa. 59:15 Truth is lacking, and whoever turns from evil is despoiled. The Lord saw it, and it displeased him that there was no justice.

Heb. 9:22 Indeed, under the law almost everything is purified with blood, and without the shedding of blood there is no forgiveness of sins.

Rom. 5:8–10 But God proves his love for us in that while we still were sinners Christ died for us. Much more surely then, now that we have been justified by his blood, will we be saved through him from the wrath of God. For if while we were enemies, we were reconciled to God through the death of his Son, much more surely, having been reconciled, will we be saved by his life.

1 Chron. 16:33 Then shall the trees of the forest sing for joy before the LORD, for he comes to judge the earth.

Question 82. Does your forgiveness of those who have harmed you depend on their repentance?

No. I am to forgive as I have been forgiven. The gospel is the astonishing good news that while we were yet sinners Christ died for us. Just as God's forgiveness of me is unconditional, and so precedes my confession of sin and repentance, so my forgiveness of those who have harmed me does not depend on their confessing and repenting of their sin. However, when I forgive the person who has done me harm, giving up any resentment or desire to retaliate, I do not condone the harm that was done or excuse the evil of the sin.

Col. 3:13 Bear with one another and, if anyone has a complaint against another, forgive each other; just as the Lord has forgiven you, so you also must forgive.

Mark 11:25 Whenever you stand praying, forgive, if you have anything against anyone; so that your Father in heaven may also forgive you your trespasses.

Col. 2:13 When you were dead in trespasses and the uncircumcision of your flesh, God made you alive together with him, when he forgave us all our tres-passes. . . .

Matt. 18:21–22 Then Peter came and said to him, "Lord, if another member of the church sins against me, how often should I forgive? As many as seven times?" Jesus said to him, "Not seven times, but, I tell you, seventy-seven times."

Heb. 12:14 Pursue peace with everyone, and the holiness without which no one will see the Lord.

Question 83. How can you forgive those who have really hurt you?

I cannot love my enemies, I cannot pray for those who persecute me, I cannot even be ready to forgive those who have really hurt me, without the grace that comes from above. I cannot be conformed to the image of God's Son, apart from the power of God's Word and Spirit. Yet I am promised that I can do all things through Christ who strengthens me.

Luke 6:27–28 But I say to you that listen, Love your enemies, do good to those who hate you, bless those who curse you, pray for those who abuse you.

James 1:17 Every generous act of giving, with every perfect gift, is from above, coming down from the Father of lights, with whom there is no variation or shadow due to change.

Rom. 8:29 For those whom he foreknew he also predestined to be conformed to the image of his Son, in order that he might be the firstborn within a large family.

Phil. 4:13 I can do all things through him who strengthens me.

Question 84. What do you mean when you speak of "the resurrection of the body"?

Because Christ lives, we will live also. The resurrection of the body celebrates our eternal value to God as living persons, each one with a unique and distinctive identity. Indeed, the living Savior who goes before us was once heard, seen, and touched in person, after the discovery of his empty tomb. The resurrection of the body means hope for the whole person, because it is in the unity of body and soul, not in soul alone, that I belong in life and in death to my faithful Savior Jesus Christ.

John 14:19 In a little while the world will no longer see me, but you will see me; because I live, you also will live.

John 11:25 Jesus said to her, "I am the resurrection and the life. Those who believe in me, even though they die, will live. . . ."

Rom. 6:5 For if we have been united with him in a death like his, we will certainly be united with him in a resurrection like his.

1 Cor. 15:21 For since death came through a human being, the resurrection of the dead has also come through a human being. . . .

1 Cor. 15:42 So it is with the resurrection of the dead. What is sown is perishable, what is raised is imperishable.

Col. 1:18 He is the head of the body, the church; he is the beginning, the firstborn from the dead, so that he might come to have first place in everything.

Question 85. What is the nature of resurrection hope?

Resurrection hope is a hope for the transformation of this world, not a hope for escape from it. It is the hope that evil in all its forms will be utterly eradicated, that past history will be redeemed, and that all the things that ever were will be made new. It is the hope of a new creation, a new heaven, and a new earth, in which God is really honored as God, human beings are truly loving, and peace and justice reign on earth.

Isa. 11:6 The wolf shall live with the lamb, the leopard shall lie down with the kid, the calf and the lion and the fatling together, and a little child shall lead them.

Rev. 21:1 Then I saw a new heaven and a new earth; for the first heaven and the first earth had passed away, and the sea was no more.

Isa. 65:17 For I am about to create new heavens and a new earth; the former things shall not be remembered or come to mind.

2 Peter 3:13 But, in accordance with his promise, we wait for new heavens and a new earth, where righteousness is at home.

2 Cor. 5:17 So if anyone is in Christ, there is a new creation: everything old has passed away; see, everything has become new!

Question 86. Does resurrection hope mean that we don't have to take action to relieve the suffering of this world?

No. When the great hope is truly alive, small hopes arise even now for alleviating the sufferings of the present time. Reconciliation—with God, with one another, and with oneself—is the great hope God has given to the world. While we commit to God the needs of the whole world in our prayers, we also know that we are commissioned to be instruments of God's peace. When hostility, injustice, and suffering are overcome here and now, we anticipate the end of all things—the life that God brings out of death, which is the meaning of resurrection hope.

> *Ps. 27:13* I believe that I shall see the goodness of the LORD in the land of the living.

> *Ps. 33:20–22* Our soul waits for the LORD; he is our help and shield. Our heart is glad in him, because we trust in his holy name. Let your steadfast love, O Lord, be upon us, even as we hope in you.

> *Rom. 14:19* Let us then pursue what makes for peace and for mutual upbuilding.

> *Deut. 30:19* I call heaven and earth to witness against you today that I have set before you life and death, blessings and curses. Choose life so that you and your descendants may live. . . .

> *Luke 1:78–79* By the tender mercy of our God, the dawn from on high will break upon us, to give light to those who sit in darkness and in the shadow of death, to guide our feet into the way of peace.

Question 87. What do you affirm when you speak of "the life everlasting"?

That God does not will to be God without us, but instead grants to us creatures—fallen and mortal as we are—eternal life. Communion with Jesus Christ is eternal life itself. In him we were chosen before the foundation of the world. By him the eternal covenant with Israel was taken up, embodied, and fulfilled. To him we are joined by the Holy Spirit through faith and adopted as children, the sons and daughters of God. Through him we are raised from death to new life. For him we shall live to all eternity.

John 3:16 For God so loved the world that he gave his only Son, so that everyone who believes in him may not perish but may have eternal life.

John 6:54 Those who eat my flesh and drink my blood have eternal life, and I will raise them up on the last day. . . .

John 17:3 And this is eternal life, that they may know you, the only true God, and Jesus Christ whom you have sent.

Rom. 6:22 But now that you have been freed from sin and enslaved to God, the advantage you get is sanctification. The end is eternal life.

Rom. 6:23 For the wages of sin is death, but the free gift of God is eternal life in Christ Jesus our Lord.

1 John 2:25 And this is what he has promised us, eternal life.

Matt. 25:34 Then the king will say to those at his right hand, "Come, you that are blessed by my Father, inherit the kingdom prepared for you from the foundation of the world. . . . "

Question 88. Won't heaven be a boring place?

No. Heaven is our true home, a world of love. There the Spirit shall be poured out into every heart in perfect love. There the Father and the Son are united in the loving bond of the Spirit. There we shall be united with them and one another. There we shall at last see face to face what we now only glimpse as through a distant mirror. Our deepest, truest delights in this life are only a dim foreshadowing of the delights that await us in heaven. "You show me the path of life. In your presence there is fullness of joy; in your right hand are pleasures forevermore" (Ps. 16:11).

John 14:2–3 In my Father's house there are many dwelling places. If it were not so, would I have told you that I go to prepare a place for you? And if I go and prepare a place for you, I will come again and will take you to myself, so that where I am, there you may be also.

Matt. 6:20 But store up for yourselves treasures in heaven, where neither moth nor rust consumes and where thieves do not break in and steal.

Matt. 8:11 I tell you, many will come from east and west and will eat with Abraham and Isaac and Jacob in the kingdom of heaven. . . .

Col. 1:5 . . . because of the hope laid up for you in heaven. You have heard of this hope before in the word of the truth, the gospel. . . .

1 Cor. 13:12 For now we see in a mirror, dimly, but then we will see face to face. Now I know only in part; then I will know fully, even as I have been fully known.

II. The Ten Commandments

Question 89. What are the Ten Commandments?

The Ten Commandments give a summary of God's law for our lives. They teach us how to live rightly with God and one another.

Deut. 10:4 Then he wrote on the tablets the same words as before, the ten commandments that the LORD had spoken to you on the mountain out of the fire on the day of the assembly; and the LORD gave them to me.

Matt. 19:17 And he said to him, "Why do you ask me about what is good? There is only one who is good. If you wish to enter into life, keep the commandments."

Question 90. Why did God give this law?

After rescuing the people of Israel from their slavery in Egypt, God led them to Mount Sinai, where they received the law through Moses. It was the great charter of liberty for Israel, a people chosen to live in covenant with God and to serve as a light to the nations. It remains the charter of liberty for all who would love, know, and serve the Lord today.

Ex. 20:2 I am the LORD your God, who brought you out of the land of Egypt, out of the house of slavery. . . .

Deut. 11:1 You shall love the LORD your God, therefore, and keep his charge, his decrees, his ordinances, and his commandments always.

Luke 1:74–75 . . . that we, being rescued from the hands of our enemies, might serve him without fear, in holiness and righteousness before him all our days.

Question 91. Why should you obey this law?

Not to win God's love, for God already loves me. Not to earn my salvation, for Christ has earned it for me. Not to avoid being punished, for then I would obey out of fear. With gladness in my heart I should obey God's law out of gratitude, for God has blessed me by it and given it for my well-being.

Ps. 118:1 O give thanks to the LORD, for he is good; his steadfast love endures forever!

Col. 3:17 And whatever you do, in word or deed, do everything in the name of the Lord Jesus, giving thanks to God the Father through him.

Question 92. What are the uses of God's law?

God's law has three uses. First, it shows me how grievously I fail to live according to God's will, driving me to pray for God's mercy. Second, it functions to restrain even the worst of sinners through the fear of punishment. Finally, it teaches me how to live a life which bears witness to the gospel, and spurs me on to do so.

Rom. 3:20 For "no human being will be justified in his sight" by deeds prescribed by the law, for through the law comes the knowledge of sin.

Rom. 7:7 What then should we say? That the law is sin? By no means! Yet, if it had not been for the law, I would not have known sin. I would not have known what it is to covet if the law had not said, "You shall not covet."

Prov. 6:23 For the commandment is a lamp and the teaching a light, and the reproofs of discipline are the way of life. . . .

Phil. 1:27a Only, live your life in a manner worthy of the gospel of Christ. . . .

Question 93. What is the first commandment?

"You shall have no other gods before me" (Ex. 20:3; Deut. 5:7).

Deut. 26:17 Today you have obtained the LORD's agreement: to be your God; and for you to walk in his ways, to keep his statutes, his commandments, and his ordinances, and to obey him.

Matt. 4:10 Jesus said to him, "Away with you, Satan! for it is written, 'Worship the Lord your God, and serve only him.'"

Question 94. What do you learn from this commandment?

No loyalty comes before my loyalty to God. I should worship and serve only God, expect all good from God alone, and love, fear, and honor God with all my heart.

Matt. 6:24 No one can serve two masters; for a slave will either hate the one and love the other, or be devoted to the one and despise the other. You cannot serve God and wealth.

Deut. 6:5 You shall love the LORD your God with all your heart, and with all your soul, and with all your might.

Prov. 9:10 The fear of the LORD is the beginning of wisdom, and the knowledge of the Holy One is insight.

Matt. 10:37 Whoever loves father or mother more than me is not worthy of me; and whoever loves son or daughter more than me is not worthy of me. . . .

Question 95. What is the second commandment?

"You shall not make for yourself an idol" (Ex. 20:4; Deut. 5:8).

Question 96. What do you learn from this commandment?

First, when I treat anything other than God as though it were God, I practice idolatry. Second, when I assume that my own interests are more important than anything else, I make them into idols, and in effect make an idol of myself.

Deut. 6:14 Do not follow other gods, any of the gods of the peoples who are all around you. . . .

1 John 5:21 Little children, keep yourselves from idols.

Ex. 34:14 For you shall worship no other god, because the LORD, whose name is Jealous, is a jealous God.

1 Chron. 16:26 For all the gods of the peoples are idols, but the LORD made the heavens.

Rom. 1:22–23 Claiming to be wise, they became fools; and they exchanged the glory of the immortal God for images resembling a mortal human being or birds or four-footed animals or reptiles.

Phil. 2:4 Let each of you look not to your own interests, but to the interests of others.

Question 97. What is the third commandment?

"You shall not make wrongful use of the name of the Lord your God" (Ex. 20:7; Deut. 5:11).

Question 98. What do you learn from this commandment?

I should use God's name with reverence and awe. God's name is taken in vain when used to support wrong. It is insulted when used carelessly, as in a curse or a pious cliché.

Ps. 29:2 Ascribe to the LORD the glory of his name; worship the Lord in holy splendor.

Rev. 15:3–4 And they sing the song of Moses, the servant of God, and the song of the Lamb: "Great and amazing are your deeds, Lord God the Almighty! Just and true are your ways, King of the nations! Lord, who will not fear and glorify your name? For you alone are holy. All nations will come and worship before you, for your judgements have been revealed,"

Ps. 138:2 I bow down toward your holy temple and give thanks to your name for your steadfast love and your faithfulness; for you have exalted your name and your word above everything.

Eph. 4:29 Let no evil talk come out of your mouths, but only what is useful for building up, as there is need, so that your words may give grace to those who hear.

Ps. 103:1–2 Bless the LORD, O my soul, and all that is within me, bless his holy name. Bless the LORD, O my soul, and do not forget all his benefits. . . .

Question 99. What is the fourth commandment?

"Remember the Sabbath day, and keep it holy" (Ex. 20:8; Deut. 5:12).

Question 100. What do you learn from this commandment?

God requires a special day to be set apart so that worship can be at the center of my life. It is right to honor God with thanks and praise, and to hear and receive God's Word, so that I may have it in my heart and on my lips, and put it into practice in my life.

Rom. 10:8 But what does it say? "The word is near you, on your lips and in your heart" (that is, the word of faith that we proclaim). . . .

Deut. 5:12 Observe the sabbath day and keep it holy, as the LORD your God commanded you.

Gen. 2:3 So God blessed the seventh day and hallowed it, because on it God rested from all the work that he had done in creation.

Lev. 23:3 Six days shall work be done; but the seventh day is a sabbath of complete rest, a holy convocation; you shall do no work: it is a sabbath to the LORD throughout your settlements.

Acts 2:42, 46 They devoted themselves to the apostles' teaching and fellowship, to the breaking of bread and the prayers. . . . Day by day, as they spent much time together in the temple, they broke bread at home and ate their food with glad and generous hearts. . . .

Question 101. Why set aside one day a week as a day of rest?

First, working people should not be taken advantage of by their employers (Deut. 5:14). My job should not be my tyrant, for my life is more than my work. Second, God requires me to put time aside for the regular study of Holy Scripture and for prayer, not only by myself but also with others, not least those in my own household.

Deut. 5:14 But the seventh day is a sabbath to the LORD your God; you shall not do any work—you, or your son or your daughter, or your male or female slave, or your ox or your donkey, or any of your livestock, or the resident alien in your towns, so that your male and female slave may rest as well as you.

Ex. 31:17 It is a sign forever between me and the people of Israel that in six days the LORD made heaven and earth, and on the seventh day he rested, and was refreshed.

Question 102. Why do we Christians usually gather on the first day of the week?

In worshiping together on the first day of the week, we celebrate our Lord's resurrection, so that the new life Christ brought us might begin to fill our whole lives.

Mark 16:2 And very early on the first day of the week, when the sun had risen, they went to the tomb.

Acts 20:7 On the first day of the week, when we met to break bread, Paul was holding a discussion with them; since he intended to leave the next day, he continued speaking until midnight.

Acts 4:33 With great power the apostles gave their testimony to the resurrection of the Lord Jesus, and great grace was upon them all.

Question 103. What is the best summary of the first four commandments?

These teach me how to live rightly with God. Jesus summed them up with the commandment he called the first and greatest: "You shall love the Lord your God with all your heart, and with all your soul, and with all your mind" (Matt. 22:37; Deut. 6:5).

Question 104. What is the fifth commandment?

"Honor your father and your mother" (Ex. 20:12; Deut. 5:16).

Question 105. What do you learn from this commandment?

Though I owe reverence to God alone, I owe genuine respect to my parents, both my mother and father. God wills me to listen to them, be thankful for the benefits I receive from them, and be considerate of their needs, especially in old age.

Eph. 5:21 Be subject to one another out of reverence for Christ.

Rom. 12:10 Love one another with mutual affection; outdo one another in showing honor.

Eph. 6:2 "Honor your father and mother"—this is the first commandment with a promise. . . .

Prov. 1:8 Hear, my child, your father's instruction, and do not reject your mother's teaching. . . .

Lev. 19:32 You shall rise before the aged, and defer to the old; and you shall fear your God: I am the LORD.

Luke 2:51 Then he went down with them and came to Nazareth, and was obedient to them. His mother treasured all these things in her heart.

Question 106. Are there limits to your obligation to obey them?

Yes. No mere human being is God. Blind obedience is not required, for everything should be tested by loyalty and obedience to God. When it seems as though I should not obey, I should always be alert to possible self-deception on my part and should pray that we may all walk in the truth of God's will.

1 Peter 2:17 Honor everyone. Love the family of believers. Fear God. Honor the emperor.

Acts 5:29 But Peter and the apostles answered, "We must obey God rather than any human authority."

Question 107. What is the sixth commandment?

"You shall not murder" (Ex. 20:13; Deut. 5:17).

Question 108. What do you learn from this commandment?

God forbids anything that harms my neighbor unfairly. Murder or injury can be done not only by direct violence but also by an angry word or a clever plan, and not only by an individual but also by unjust social institutions. I should honor every human being, including my enemy, as a person made in God's image.

1 John 3:15 All who hate a brother or sister are murderers, and you know that murderers do not have eternal life abiding in them.

Prov. 24:17 Do not rejoice when your enemies fall, and do not let your heart be glad when they stumble. . . .

Rom. 12:19–20 Beloved, never avenge yourselves, but leave room for the wrath of God; for it is written, "Vengeance is mine, I will repay, says the Lord." No, "if your enemies are hungry, feed them; if they are thirsty, give them something to drink; for by doing this you will heap burning coals on their heads."

Col. 3:12–13 As God's chosen ones, holy and beloved, clothe yourselves with compassion, kindness, humility, meekness, and patience. Bear with one another and, if anyone has a complaint against another, forgive each other; just as the Lord has forgiven you, so you also must forgive.

Matt. 5:21–22 You have heard that it was said to those of ancient times, "You shall not murder"; and "whoever murders shall be liable to judgment." But I say to you that if you are angry with a brother or sister, you will be liable to judgment; and if you insult a brother or sister, you will be liable to the council; and if you say, "You fool," you will be liable to the hell of fire.

Matt. 26:52 Then Jesus said to him, "Put your sword back into its place; for all who take the sword will perish by the sword."

Question 109. What is the seventh commandment?

"You shall not commit adultery" (Ex. 20:14; Deut. 5:18).

Question 110. What do you learn from this commandment?

God requires fidelity and purity in sexual relations. Since love is God's great gift, God expects me not to corrupt it, or confuse it with momentary desire or the selfish fulfillment of my own pleasures. God forbids all sexual immorality, whether in married or in single life.

Eph. 5:3 But fornication and impurity of any kind, or greed, must not even be mentioned among you, as is proper among saints.

Matt. 5:27–29 You have heard that it was said, "You shall not commit adultery." But I say to you that everyone who looks at a woman with lust has already committed adultery with her in his heart. If your right eye causes you to sin, tear it out and throw it away; it is better for you to lose one of your members than for your whole body to be thrown into hell.

Heb. 13:4 Let marriage be held in honor by all, and let the marriage bed be kept undefiled; for God will judge fornicators and adulterers.

1 Thess. 4:3–4 For this is the will of God, your sanctification: that you abstain from fornication; that each one of you know how to control your own body in holiness and honor. . . .

Question 111. What is the eighth commandment?

"You shall not steal" (Ex. 20:15; Deut. 5:19).

Question 112. What do you learn from this commandment?

God forbids all theft and robbery, including schemes, tricks, or systems that unjustly take what belongs to someone else. God requires me not to be driven by greed, not to misuse or waste the gifts I have been given, and not to distrust the promise that God will supply my needs.

Job 20:19–20 For they have crushed and abandoned the poor, they have seized a house that they did not build. "They knew no quiet in their bellies; in their greed they let nothing escape."

Jer. 22:13 Woe to him who builds his house by unrighteousness, and his upper rooms by injustice; who makes his neighbors work for nothing, and does not give them their wages. . . .

Prov. 18.9 One who is slack in work is close kin to a vandal.

1 Tim. 6:9–10 But those who want to be rich fall into temptation and are trapped by many senseless and harmful desires that plunge people into ruin and destruction. For the love of money is the root of all kinds of evil, and in their eagerness to be rich some have wandered away from the faith and pierced themselves with many pains.

1 John 3:17 How does God's love abide in anyone who has the world's goods and sees a brother or sister in need and yet refuses help?

Luke 12:15 And he said to them, "Take care! Be on your guard against all kinds of greed; for one's life does not consist in the abundance of possessions."

Phil. 4:19 And my God will fully satisfy every need of yours according to his riches in glory in Christ Jesus.

Question 113. What is the ninth commandment?

"You shall not bear false witness against your neighbor" (Ex. 20:16; Deut. 5:20).

Question 114. What do you learn from this commandment?

God forbids me to damage the honor or reputation of my neighbor. I should not say false things against anyone for the sake of money, favor, or friendship, for the sake of revenge, or for any other reason. God requires me to speak the truth, to speak well of my neighbor when I can, and to view the faults of my neighbor with tolerance when I cannot.

> *Zech. 8:16–17* These are the things that you shall do: Speak the truth to one another, render in your gates judgments that are true and make for peace, do not devise evil in your hearts against one another, and love no false oath; for all these are things that I hate, says the LORD.
>
> *1 Peter 3:16* Keep your conscience clear, so that, when you are maligned, those who abuse you for your good conduct in Christ may be put to shame.
>
> *Prov. 14:5* A faithful witness does not lie, but a false witness breathes out lies.
>
> *James 4:11* Do not speak evil against one another, brothers and sisters. Whoever speaks evil against another or judges another, speaks evil against the law and judges the law; but if you judge the law, you are not a doer of the law but a judge.
>
> *1 Peter 4:8* Above all, maintain constant love for one another, for love covers a multitude of sins.

Question 115. Does this commandment forbid racism and other forms of negative stereotyping?

Yes. In forbidding false witness against my neighbor, God forbids me to be prejudiced against people who belong to any vulnerable, different, or disfavored social group. Jews, women, homosexuals, racial and ethnic minorities, and national enemies are among those who have suffered terribly from being subjected to the slurs of social prejudice. Negative stereotyping is a form of falsehood that invites actions of humiliation, abuse, and violence as forbidden by the commandment against murder.

Rom. 3:13, 15 "Their throats are opened graves; they use their tongues to deceive." "The venom of vipers is under their lips." . . . "Their feet are swift to shed blood."

Prov. 31:8–9 Speak out for those who cannot speak, for the rights of all the destitute. Speak out, judge righteously, defend the rights of the poor and needy.

Matt. 7:1–2 Do not judge, so that you may not be judged. For with the judgment you make you will be judged, and the measure you give will be the measure you get.

Question 116. What is the tenth commandment?

"You shall not covet what is your neighbor's" (Ex. 20:17; Deut. 5:21).

Question 117. What do you learn from this commandment?

My whole heart should belong to God alone, not to money or the things of this world. "Coveting" means desiring something wrongfully. I should not resent the good fortune or success of my neighbor or allow envy to corrupt my heart.

Heb. 13:5 Keep your lives free from the love of money, and be content with what you have; for he has said, "I will never leave you or forsake you."

Gal. 5:26 Let us not become conceited, competing against one another, envying one another.

Question 118. What is the best summary of the last six commandments?

These teach me how to live rightly with my neighbor. Jesus summed them up with the commandment which is like the greatest one about loving God: "You shall love your neighbor as yourself" (Matt. 22:39; Lev. 19:18).

Question 119. Can you obey these commandments perfectly?

No. I am at once a *forgiven* sinner and a forgiven *sinner*. As a sinner without excuse, I fail to obey these commandments as God requires. "For whoever keeps the whole law but fails in one point has become accountable for all of it" (James 2:10). I should not adjust the law to my failures, nor reduce my failures before God. Yet there is more grace in God than sin in me. While I should not cease to pray to God for mercy, I can be confident that God is forgiving and that I will be set free from all my sins. By grace I can confess my sins, repent of them, and grow in love and knowledge day by day.

Ps. 14:3 They have all gone astray, they are all alike perverse; there is no one who does good, no, not one.

Eph. 2:8 For by grace you have been saved through faith, and this is not your own doing; it is the gift of God. . . .

Ps. 130:3–4 If you, O LORD, should mark iniquities, Lord, who could stand? But there is forgiveness with you, so that you may be revered.

Col. 1:13–14 He has rescued us from the power of darkness and transferred us into the kingdom of his beloved Son, in whom we have redemption, the forgiveness of sins.

1 John 1:8 If we say that we have no sin, we deceive ourselves, and the truth is not in us.

III. The Lord's Prayer

Question 120. What is prayer?

Prayer means calling upon God whose Spirit is always present with us. In prayer we approach God with reverence, confidence, and humility. Prayer involves both addressing God in praise, confession, thanksgiving, and supplication, and listening for God's word within our hearts. When we adore God, we are filled with wonder, love, and praise before God's heavenly glory, not least when we find it hidden in the cross of Golgotha. When confessing our guilt to God, we ask for forgiveness with humble and sorry hearts, remembering that God is gracious as well as holy. When giving thanks to God, we acknowledge God's great goodness, rejoicing in God for all that is so wonderfully provided for us. Finally, when calling upon God to hear our requests, we affirm that God draws near in every need and sorrow of life, and ask God to do so again.

Ps. 48.1 Great is the LORD and greatly to be praised in the city of our God.

Ps. 96:8–9 Ascribe to the LORD the glory due his name; bring an offering, and come into his courts. Worship the Lord in holy splendor; tremble before him, all the earth.

James 5:16 Therefore confess your sins to one another, and pray for one another, so that you may be healed. The prayer of the righteous is powerful and effective.

1 John 1:9 If we confess our sins, he who is faithful and just will forgive us our sins and cleanse us from all unrighteousness.

Ps. 107:8 Let them thank the LORD for his steadfast love, for his wonderful works to humankind.

Ps. 75:1 We give thanks to you, O God; we give thanks; your name is near. People tell of your wondrous deeds.

Ps. 50:15 Call on me in the day of trouble; I will deliver you, and you shall glorify me.

Ps. 145:18 The LORD is near to all who call on him, to all who call on him in truth.

Eph. 6:18 Pray in the Spirit at all times in every prayer and supplication. To that end keep alert and always persevere in supplication for all the saints.

Question 121. What is the purpose of prayer?

Prayer brings us into communion with God. The more our lives are rooted in prayer, the more we sense how wonderful God is in grace, purity, majesty, and love. Prayer means offering our lives completely to God, submitting ourselves to God's will, and waiting faithfully for God's grace. Through prayer God frees us from anxiety, equips us for service, and deepens our faith.

Ps. 62:8 Trust in him at all times, O people; pour out your heart before him; God is a refuge for us.

Ps. 139:1 O LORD, you have searched me and known me.

Phil. 4:6 Do not worry about anything, but in everything by prayer and supplication with thanksgiving let your requests be made known to God.

Matt. 7:7–8 Ask, and it will be given you; search, and you will find; knock, and the door will be opened for you. For everyone who asks receives, and everyone who searches finds, and for everyone who knocks, the door will be opened.

Question 122. How does God respond to our prayers?

God takes all our prayers into account, weighing them with divine wisdom, and responding to them by a perfect will. Although for the time being God's answers may seem beyond our understanding, or sometimes even bitter, we know nonetheless that they are always determined by the grace of our Lord Jesus Christ. God answers our prayers, particularly for temporal blessings, only in ways that are compatible with the larger purposes of God's glory and our salvation. Communion with God is finally the answer within the answers to all our prayers.

1 John 5:14 This is the boldness we have in him, that if we ask anything according to his will, he hears us.

James 1:17 Every generous act of giving, with every perfect gift, is from above, coming down from the Father of lights, with whom there is no variation or shadow due to change.

Matt. 6:33 But strive first for the kingdom of God and his righteousness, and all these things will be given to you as well.

Question 123. What encourages us to pray each day?

The God who has adopted us as children is the God who encourages and commands us to pray. When we pray, we respond with love to that greater love which meets us from above. Before we enter into prayer, God is ready to grant all that we need. We may turn to God with confidence each day, not because we are worthy, but simply because of God's grace. By praying we acknowledge that we depend on grace for all that is good, beautiful, life-giving, and true.

Isa. 65:24 Before they call I will answer, while they are yet speaking I will hear.

Luke 11:12–13 Or if the child asks for an egg, will [you] give a scorpion? If you then, who are evil, know how to give good gifts to your children, how much more will the heavenly Father give the Holy Spirit to those who ask him!

Phil. 4:8 Finally, beloved, whatever is true, whatever is honorable, whatever is just, whatever is pure, whatever is pleasing, whatever is commendable, if there is any excellence and if there is anything worthy of praise, think about these things.

Eph. 3:20–21 Now to him who by the power at work within us is able to accomplish abundantly far more than all we can ask or imagine, to him be glory in the church and in Christ Jesus to all generations, forever and ever. Amen.

Question 124. What prayer serves as our rule or pattern?

Our rule or pattern is found in the Lord's Prayer, which Jesus taught to his disciples:

Our Father in heaven,
hallowed be your name,
your kingdom come,
your will be done,
on earth as in heaven.
Give us today our daily bread.
Forgive us our sins
as we forgive those who sin against us.
Save us from the time of trial
and deliver us from evil.
For the kingdom, the power, and the
glory are yours now and for ever. Amen.

These words express everything that we may desire and expect from God.

Question 125. What is the design of the Lord's Prayer?

The Lord's Prayer falls into two parts, preceded by an opening address, and concluded by a "doxology" or word of praise. Each part consists of three petitions. The first part concerns God's glory; the second part, our salvation. The first part involves our love for God; the second part, God's love for us. The petitions in part one will not be fulfilled perfectly until the life to come; those in part two relate more directly to our present needs here and now.

Question 126. What is meant by addressing God as "Our Father in heaven"?

By addressing God as "our Father," we draw near with childlike reverence and place ourselves securely in God's hands. Although God is certainly everywhere, God is said to exist and dwell "in heaven." For while God is free to enter into the closest relationship with the creature, God does not belong to the order of created beings. "Heaven" is the seat of divine authority, the place from which God reigns in glory and brings salvation to earth. Our opening address expresses our confidence that we rest securely in God's intimate care and that nothing on earth lies beyond the reach of God's grace.

Rom. 8:15 For you did not receive a spirit of slavery to fall back into fear, but you have received a spirit of adoption. When we cry, "Abba! Father!" it is that very Spirit bearing witness with our spirit that we are children of God. . . .

Jer. 23:23–24 Am I a God near by, says the LORD, and not a God far off? Who can hide in secret places so that I cannot see them? says the LORD. Do I not fill heaven and earth? says the LORD.

Acts 17:24–25 The God who made the world and everything in it, he who is Lord of heaven and earth, does not live in shrines made by human hands, nor is he served by human hands, as though he needed anything, since he himself gives to all mortals life and breath and all things.

Question 127. What is meant by the first petition, "Hallowed be your name"?

This petition is placed first, because it comprehends the goal and purpose of the whole prayer. The glory of God's name is the highest concern in all that we pray and do. God's "name" stands for God's being as well as for God's attributes and works. When we pray for this name to be "hallowed," we ask that we and all others will know and glorify God as God really is and that all things will be so ordered that they serve God truly for God's sake.

Jer. 9:23–24 Thus says the LORD: Do not let the wise boast in their wisdom, do not let the mighty boast in their might, do not let the wealthy boast in their wealth; but let those who boast boast in this, that they understand and know me, that I am the LORD; I act with steadfast love, justice, and righteousness in the earth, for in these things I delight, says the LORD.

Rom. 11:36 For from him and through him and to him are all things. To him be the glory forever. Amen.

Ps. 115:1 Not to us, O LORD, not to us, but to your name give glory, for the sake of your steadfast love and your faithfulness.

Question 128. What is meant by the second petition, "Your kingdom come"?

We are asking God to come and rule among us through faith, love, and justice—and not through any one of them without the others. We pray for both the church and the world, that God will rule in our hearts through faith, in our personal relationships through love, and in our institutional affairs through justice. We ask especially that the gospel will not be withheld from us, but rightly preached and received. We pray that the church will be upheld and increase, particularly when in distress; and that all the world will more and more submit to God's reign, until that day when crying and pain are no more, and we live forever with God in perfect peace.

Ps. 68:1 Let God rise up, let his enemies be scattered; let those who hate him flee before him.

2 Thess. 3:1 Finally, brothers and sisters, pray for us, so that the word of the Lord may spread rapidly and be glorified everywhere, just as it is among you. . . .

Rev. 22:20 The one who testifies to these things says, "Surely I am coming soon." Amen. Come, Lord Jesus!

Rom. 8:22–24 We know that the whole creation has been groaning in labor pains until now; and not only the creation, but we ourselves, who have the first fruits of the Spirit, groan inwardly while we wait for adoption, the redemption of our bodies. For in hope we were saved. Now hope that is seen is not hope. For who hopes for what is seen?

1 Cor. 15:20, 28 But in fact Christ has been raised from the dead, the first fruits of those who have died. . . . When all things are subjected to him, then the Son himself will also be subjected to the one who put all things in subjection under him, so that God may be all in all.

Question 129. What is meant by the third petition, "Your will be done, on earth as in heaven"?

Of course, God's will is always done and will surely come to pass, whether we desire it or not. But the phrase "on earth as in heaven" means that we ask for the grace to do God's will on earth in the way that it is done in heaven—gladly and from the heart. We thus ask that all opposition to God's will might be removed from the earth, and especially from our own hearts. We ask for the freedom to conform our desires and deeds more fully to God's, so that we might be completely delivered from our sin. We yield ourselves, in life and in death, to God's will.

Ps. 119:34–36 Give me understanding, that I may keep your law and observe it with my whole heart. Lead me in the path of your commandments, for I delight in it. Turn my heart to your decrees, and not to selfish gain.

Ps. 103:20, 22 Bless the LORD, O you his angels, you mighty ones who do his bidding, obedient to his spoken word. . . . Bless the LORD, all his works, in all places of his dominion. Bless the LORD, O my soul.

Luke 22:42 Father, if you are willing, remove this cup from me; yet, not my will but yours be done.

Rom. 12:2 Do not be conformed to this world, but be transformed by the renewing of your minds, so that you may discern what is the will of God—what is good and acceptable and perfect.

Question 130. What is meant by the fourth petition, "Give us today our daily bread"?

We ask God to provide for all our needs, for we know that God, who cares for us in every area of our life, has promised us temporal as well as spiritual blessings. God commands us to pray each day for all that we need and no more, so that we will learn to rely completely on God. We pray that we will use what we are given wisely, remembering especially the poor and the needy. Along with every living creature we look to God, the source of all generosity, to bless us and nourish us, according to the divine good pleasure.

Prov. 30:8 Remove far from me falsehood and lying; give me neither poverty nor riches; feed me with the food that I need. . . .

Ps. 90:17 Let the favor of the Lord our God be upon us, and prosper for us the work of our hands—O prosper the work of our hands!

Ps. 55:22 Cast your burden on the LORD, and he will sustain you; he will never permit the righteous to be moved.

Ps. 72:4 May he defend the cause of the poor of the people, give deliverance to the needy, and crush the oppressor.

Ps. 104:27–28 These all look to you to give them their food in due season; when you give to them, they gather it up; when you open your hand, they are filled with good things.

Question 131. What is meant by the fifth petition, "Forgive us our sins as we forgive those who sin against us"?

We pray that a new and right spirit will be put within us. We ask for the grace to treat others, especially those who harm us, with the same mercy that we have received from God. We remember that not one day goes by when we do not need to turn humbly to God for our own forgiveness. We know that our reception of this forgiveness can be blocked by our unwillingness to forgive others. We ask that we will not delight in doing evil, nor in avenging any wrong, but that we will survive all cruelty without bitterness and overcome evil with good, so that our hearts will be knit together with the mercy and forgiveness of God.

Matt. 18:33 Should you not have had mercy on your fellow slave, as I had mercy on you?

Matt. 6:14–15 For if you forgive others their trespasses, your heavenly Father will also forgive you; but if you do not forgive others, neither will your Father forgive your trespasses.

Ps. 51:10 Create in me a clean heart, O God, and put a new and right spirit within me.

1 John 2:1–2 My little children, I am writing these things to you so that you may not sin. But if anyone does sin, we have an advocate with the Father, Jesus Christ the righteous; and he is the atoning sacrifice for our sins, and not for ours only but also for the sins of the whole world.

Question 132. What is meant by the final petition, "Save us from the time of trial and deliver us from evil"?

We ask God to protect us from our own worst impulses and from all external powers of destruction in the world. We ask that we might not yield to despair in the face of seemingly hopeless circumstances. We pray for the grace to remember and believe, despite our unbelief, that no matter how bleak the world may sometimes seem, there is nonetheless a depth of love which is deeper than our despair, and that this love—which delivered Israel from slavery in Egypt and raised our

Lord Jesus from the dead—will finally swallow up forever all that would now seem to defeat it.

2 Cor. 4:8 We are afflicted in every way, but not crushed; perplexed, but not driven to despair. . . .

Eph. 3:19 . . . and to know the love of Christ that surpasses knowledge, so that you may be filled with all the fullness of God.

Matt. 26:41 Stay awake and pray that you may not come into the time of trial; the spirit indeed is willing, but the flesh is weak.

Question 133. What is meant by the closing doxology, "For the kingdom, the power and the glory are yours now and for ever"?

We give God thanks and praise for the kingdom more powerful than all enemies, for the power perfected in the weakness of love, and for the glory that includes our well-being and that of the whole creation, both now and to all eternity. We give thanks and praise to God as made known through Christ our Lord.

Rev. 5:12 Worthy is the Lamb that was slaughtered to receive power and wealth and wisdom and might and honor and glory and blessing!

Rev. 4:11 You are worthy, our Lord and God, to receive glory and honor and power, for you created all things, and by your will they existed and were created.

1 Chron. 29:11, 13 Yours, O LORD, are the greatness, the power, the glory, the victory, and the majesty; for all that is in the heavens and on the earth is yours; yours is the kingdom, O LORD, and you are exalted as head above all. . . . And now, our God, we give thanks to you and praise your glorious name.

Question 134. What is meant by the word "Amen"?

"Amen" means "so be it" or "let it be so." It expresses our complete confidence in the triune God, the God of the covenant with Israel as fulfilled through our Lord Jesus Christ, who makes no promise that will not be kept, and whose steadfast love and mercy endures forever.

Rev. 22:20 The one who testifies to these things says, "Surely I am coming soon." Amen. Come, Lord Jesus!

2 Cor. 1:20 For in him every one of God's promises is a "Yes." For this reason it is through him that we say the "Amen," to the glory of God.

2 Tim. 2:13 If we are faithless, he remains faithful—for he cannot deny himself.